[H.A.S.C. No. 115–16]

CRAFTING AN INFORMATION WARFARE AND COUNTER–PROPAGANDA STRATEGY FOR THE EMERGING SECURITY ENVIRONMENT

HEARING

BEFORE THE

SUBCOMMITTEE ON EMERGING THREATS AND CAPABILITIES

OF THE

COMMITTEE ON ARMED SERVICES HOUSE OF REPRESENTATIVES

ONE HUNDRED FIFTEENTH CONGRESS

FIRST SESSION

HEARING HELD
MARCH 15, 2017

U.S. GOVERNMENT PUBLISHING OFFICE

25–048   WASHINGTON : 2017

For sale by the Superintendent of Documents, U.S. Government Publishing Office
Internet: bookstore.gpo.gov   Phone: toll free (866) 512–1800; DC area (202) 512–1800
Fax: (202) 512–2104   Mail: Stop IDCC, Washington, DC 20402–0001

SUBCOMMITTEE ON EMERGING THREATS AND CAPABILITIES

ELISE M. STEFANIK, New York, *Chairwoman*

BILL SHUSTER, Pennsylvania	JAMES R. LANGEVIN, Rhode Island
BRAD R. WENSTRUP, Ohio	RICK LARSEN, Washington
RALPH LEE ABRAHAM, Louisiana	JIM COOPER, Tennessee
LIZ CHENEY, Wyoming, *Vice Chair*	JACKIE SPEIER, California
JOE WILSON, South Carolina	MARC A. VEASEY, Texas
FRANK A. LoBIONDO, New Jersey	TULSI GABBARD, Hawaii
TRENT FRANKS, Arizona	BETO O'ROURKE, Texas
DOUG LAMBORN, Colorado	STEPHANIE N. MURPHY, Florida
AUSTIN SCOTT, Georgia	

KEVIN GATES, *Professional Staff Member*
LINDSAY KAVANAUGH, *Professional Staff Member*
NEVE SCHADLER, *Clerk*

CONTENTS

Page

STATEMENTS PRESENTED BY MEMBERS OF CONGRESS

Langevin, Hon. James R., a Representative from Rhode Island, Ranking Member, Subcommittee on Emerging Threats and Capabilities 13

Stefanik, Hon. Elise M., a Representative from New York, Chairwoman, Subcommittee on Emerging Threats and Capabilities 1

WITNESSES

Armstrong, Matthew, Associate Fellow, King's Centre for Strategic Communications, King's College London 3

Lumpkin, Michael D., Principal, Neptune 5

Thomas, Timothy L., Senior Analyst, Foreign Military Studies Office, Fort Leavenworth 7

APPENDIX

PREPARED STATEMENTS:
    Armstrong, Matthew 37
    Lumpkin, Michael D. 50
    Stefanik, Hon. Elise M. 35
    Thomas, Timothy L. 62

DOCUMENTS SUBMITTED FOR THE RECORD:
    [There were no Documents submitted.]

WITNESS RESPONSES TO QUESTIONS ASKED DURING THE HEARING:
    [There were no Questions submitted during the hearing.]

QUESTIONS SUBMITTED BY MEMBERS POST HEARING:
    Mr. Franks 81

CRAFTING AN INFORMATION WARFARE AND COUNTER–PROPAGANDA STRATEGY FOR THE EMERGING SECURITY ENVIRONMENT

HOUSE OF REPRESENTATIVES,
COMMITTEE ON ARMED SERVICES,
SUBCOMMITTEE ON EMERGING THREATS AND CAPABILITIES,
Washington, DC, Wednesday, March 15, 2017.

The subcommittee met, pursuant to call, at 3:16 p.m., in room 2118, Rayburn House Office Building, Hon. Elise M. Stefanik (chairwoman of the subcommittee) presiding.

OPENING STATEMENT OF HON. ELISE M. STEFANIK, A REPRESENTATIVE FROM NEW YORK, CHAIRWOMAN, SUBCOMMITTEE ON EMERGING THREATS AND CAPABILITIES

Ms. STEFANIK. The subcommittee will come to order.

I would like to welcome everyone to this hearing of the Emerging Threats and Capabilities Subcommittee of the House Armed Services Committee on the very timely topic of information warfare and counter propaganda. Although the subcommittee has met several times already in closed classified sessions, today is our first open and public hearing. As such, I would like to take a moment to welcome and thank our new and returning subcommittee members.

Our topic today is incredibly important. Cyber warfare and influence campaigns that are being waged against our country represent a national security challenge of generational proportions. In talking about influence campaigns, we too often focus on the digital and technical aspects on the internet and social media. While those aspects are critical and indeed have served as an accelerant to speed up communications and effects, we should remember to take a step back and keep in mind that information warfare is about information, not just the medium. And our understanding of this form of warfare should also include the psychological, cognitive, and cultural aspects of the messages bombarding us from all sources.

I would like to read a quote I recently reviewed. Quote, "There has never been a time in our history when there was so great a need for our citizens to be informed and to understand what is happening in the world. The cause of freedom is being challenged throughout the world today and propaganda is one of the most powerful weapons they have in this struggle. Deceit, distortion, and lies are systemically used by them as a matter of deliberate policy," end quote.

Those were the words of President Harry Truman in 1950. He spoke of a conflict of ideas that is still occurring today. And, unfortunately, it is a conflict we have largely ignored. I chose this quote as a reminder that information warfare and propaganda efforts are not new. The tools have changed, but enemy doctrine has not. Information warfare is shaping the international environment. There may not be overt and open fighting, but there is certainly open conflict.

Information warfare is being waged in an aggressive ongoing competition over territory, resources, and people in the Crimea, in the South China Sea, in Iraq, and in Syria. People are being desensitized to the reality of actions around them, increasing the likelihood of misunderstanding and miscalculation.

Our core values of truth, democratic principles, and self-determination are under assault. While the Department of Defense [DOD] plays a critical role in this form of warfare, it cannot bear responsibility alone. Countering adversarial propaganda requires a whole-of-government strategy using all instruments of national power to harness the authorities, tools, and resources required to mitigate and marginalize its harmful effects. With this in mind, the National Defense Authorization Act [NDAA] last year authorized and expanded the mission of the State Department's Global Engagement Center [GEC] to counter state-sponsored propaganda efforts such as Russia, China, Iran, and North Korea.

We look forward to continuing to work with the center and the Department of Defense this year as we craft an information warfare and counter-propaganda strategy for an emerging security environment.

Before I turn to the ranking member for his comments, I would like to highlight a few questions for our witnesses and members to consider as we proceed throughout the hearing. First, do we have an adequate strategy for countering the blatant lies and mistruths being promulgated by sophisticated nation-state actors that have both resources and political will? Second, do we truly understand the information warfare and propaganda strategies of our enemies, be they state or nonstate actors? And lastly, since the United States remains a technological leader and innovator with tremendous creativity, how do we better harness our advantages to counter our adversaries?

[The prepared statement of Ms. Stefanik can be found in the Appendix on page 35.]

Ms. STEFANIK. In the future, when the ranking member arrives, I will turn to him for his opening statements, but in the meantime, I am going to introduce our witnesses.

We welcome three distinguished witnesses here this afternoon. First, the Honorable Matt Armstrong, an associate fellow at the King's Centre for Strategic Communications, King's College London. Next, the Honorable Michael Lumpkin, formerly an Assistant Secretary of Defense and coordinator of the Global Engagement Center, now a principal at Neptune Strategies. And finally, Mr. Timothy Thomas, a senior analyst at the Foreign Military Studies Office at Fort Leavenworth, and the author of several books and articles on Russian and Chinese information operations [IO] and cyber policy, one of which I have here.

Welcome to all of our witnesses. I would like to remind you that your testimony will be included in the record, and we ask that you summarize key points from that testimony in 5 minutes or less. We will wait for Mr. Langevin's arrival, but in the meantime, Mr. Armstrong why don't you go ahead with your opening statement.

STATEMENT OF MATTHEW ARMSTRONG, ASSOCIATE FELLOW, KING'S CENTRE FOR STRATEGIC COMMUNICATIONS, KING'S COLLEGE LONDON

Mr. ARMSTRONG. Thank you. Chairwoman Stefanik, distinguished members of the subcommittee, thank you for this opportunity to speak on information warfare and countering propaganda. This is an important conversation as information and informational activities create both opportunities and threats to our Nation's physical, societal, and economic security. This is a strategic problem requiring a strategic review of not just the threat, but also of our constraints. We may develop good tactics, but any success from these will be undone if we fail to get the strategy right, as well as properly align our efforts toward our objectives. Be confident that our adversaries are doing this realignment and using our doctrine and our public writings as their starting point.

The information domain is not a nuance at the margins, but a central facet of international affairs. We have known this for a long time, even if we need constant reminding. A 1918 report by the U.S Army General Staff recognized that in the, quote, "strategic equation of war, there are four factors: Combat, economic, political, and psychologic, and that the last of these is coequal with the others," end quote.

Today, we refer to this as the DIME model of national power: diplomacy, information, military, economic. A July 1945 report from the State Department recognized that the, quote, "nature of present day foreign relations makes it essential for the United States to maintain informational activities abroad as an integral part of the conduct of our foreign affairs." Two years later, a joint congressional report elucidated on this point: "Europe today has again become a vast battlefield of ideologies in which words have replaced armaments as the active elements of attack and defense," end quote.

Today, as the traditional barriers of influence and disruption are obliterated by modern communication and transportation networks, the role of information is more important than ever.

Understanding and elevating the appreciation of the informational or psychological affect of our words and deeds can make for more effective, more enduring, and less expensive outcomes. Every situation is unique and sometimes you need to put two in the heart and one in the mind, but between increasingly transparent battlefields and adversaries intentionally operating below or outside of our escalation ladders, we must be more adept in this environment. We may call this affair information warfare, but this is too narrow and too shallow, and it inhibits appreciating the psychological affects of actions. It also encourages the false concept of a battle of narratives as if there is a magic combination of nouns and verbs that will win the day. We may use more inclusive labels, like political warfare or hybrid warfare, two terms with subtle yet possibly useful distinctions.

Putting aside the label, we fail to appreciate how the success of our adversary's propaganda supporting their agenda or targeting our activities, whether military, economic, or political, often rest on our credibility. Its effectiveness is often influenced by the degree to which people believe what we say, how much they trust what we do, and how the audience perceives the two as consistent and aligned.

Abroad, we face a situation which our adversaries are often perceived as more credible than us as they spotlight, exploit, and often outright manufacture gaps between what we say, what we do, and our national values. Proof of this is when our adversaries are given the benefit of the doubt, while our word is questioned, our actions subjected to charges of hypocrisy and aggression. This is magnified by failing to understand the local information environments.

There are several challenges hindering our credibility and the ability to be effective in today's environment. First, our messages and actions are generally disunified. We have a competitive advantage in terms of resources, people skills, and scale. Yet our various government departments and agencies are organized in such a way that makes coordination nearly impossible.

Beyond the obvious, this includes failing to understand, coordinate, or support programs that may develop and strengthen local defenses, even inoculation, against adversarial influence. Lesser known examples include fish and wildlife services, helping game wardens in Africa, exchange programs, and the U.S. Navy tenders helping local harbor masters and mechanics. And then there is the damaging divide between defense public affairs and other defense information professionals, as well as the segregation of public diplomacy inside the State Department.

The lack of coordination and bureaucratic cultural divides contribute to our second challenge, which is that our response to adversarial propaganda is almost invariably reactionary. When our adversaries explain their actions to the world or make claims about us, we find ourselves scrambling to prove them wrong. This keeps us on our heels and requires us to overcome the narrative set by others. It also means limited consideration of the psychological affect of actions, which the Chinese appear to be overcoming in their recent reorganization of their cyberspace operations forces.

The third challenge is the militarization of our foreign policy. In the absence of a clear strategy and organizing principles, the Department of Defense has by default taken the lead in much of our foreign policy efforts. The very term "strategic communication" reflects this role as it was born out of the need to fill a gap left by the State Department. But placing our military as our primary implement of foreign policy also promotes a perception that we are an insecure Nation.

We have remarkably little relevant experience in combatting the political warfare being waged against us. We may imagine that the United States Information Agency [USIA] and the Active Measures Working Group are guideposts, but they were never intended or fit for purpose for this action and they were relatively small and reactionary. Neither is a useful model for proactive and unified defense, let alone offense.

We must change our mind-set about adversarial propaganda and subversive actions, especially those carried out below or outside the military's phasing construct. This starts with changing the language we use. We need to think and speak in terms of undermining adversarial psychological influence which will guide us toward preemptive behavior and messages. We need to think and speak in terms of a communication environment which will guide us toward a preemptive interactivity that can establish, preserve, and strengthen our credibility so that we set the narrative that must be displaced by our adversaries. We must think about why adversarial propaganda has traction, and accept that we cannot bomb our way to success. We must organize in a way that aligns our efforts for credible, smart, preemptive action and swift, credible, trusted reactions.

In addition to internal reorganizations addressing cultural divides, departments and agencies beyond Department of Defense and State bring skills and expertise to this struggle.

I am thankful that this committee has convened this hearing as I am thankful for past amendments from this committee that have affected the State Department, but in many ways this discussion is happening in a vacuum. Are other committees exercising their oversight to inquire about this topic, set priorities, or hold their respective departments and agencies accountable? And we must understand the role of society in our foreign policy and the permeability of our borders and the marketplace of loyalty, which I described elsewhere. There is a vulnerability, not just political support for our efforts, but what might be considered within organizational security parlance as insider threats. Consider Major Nidal Hasan, Jihad Jane, and other so-called lone wolves who are inspired often through sympathy or empathy with our adversaries.

I will close with another quote, this one from 1963: "Some day, this Nation will recognize that global nonmilitary conflict must be pursued with the same intensity and preparation as global military conflicts." Unfortunately, that day has yet to come, but I hope this hearing is the start of setting us on the right path. Continuing to get this wrong is a threat to our national security, to our economic growth, and to our very standing as a world leader.

Thank you again for the opportunity to discuss this important topic. I look forward to your questions.

[The prepared statement of Mr. Armstrong can be found in the Appendix on page 37.]

Ms. STEFANIK. Thank you, Mr. Armstrong.

Mr. Lumpkin.

STATEMENT OF MICHAEL D. LUMPKIN, PRINCIPAL, NEPTUNE

Mr. LUMPKIN. Chairwoman Stefanik, Ranking Member Langevin, and distinguished members of the committee, thank you for the opportunity to be here today as a private citizen in an individual capacity. Thank you very much.

I trust my experience as a career special operations officer, Assistant Secretary of Defense for Special Operations, and special envoy and coordinator at the Global Engagement Center will be helpful in providing perspective on the current state of the U.S. Government's [USG's] strategy, capabilities, and direction in information warfare and counterpropaganda.

The previous administration and the 114th Congress demonstrated clear commitment to this issue, as evidenced by President

Obama's executive order that established the Global Engagement Center and the 2017 National Defense Authorization Act that expanded the center's mission.

The NDAA expanded the GEC's mandate to include counter-state propaganda, as Chairwoman Stefanik mentioned, and disinformation efforts. This is well beyond the original charter which limited it to diminishing the influence of terrorist organizations such as the Islamic State of Iraq and Syria [ISIS] in this information domain. This is a big step in the right direction, but the sobering fact is that we are still far from where we ultimately need to be to operate in the modern information environment.

As I said, I am very pleased to be joined by Matt and Tim, two of the most experienced people in this space, who I think collectively, we should be able to answer most of this committee's questions.

Since the end of the Cold War with the Soviet Union, which was largely—arguably, the last period in history when the U.S. successfully engaged in sustained information warfare and counter-state propaganda efforts, technology and how the world communicates has drastically changed. We now live in a hyperconnected world where the flow of information moves in real time. The lines of authority and effort between public diplomacy, public affairs, and information warfare have blurred to the point where, in many cases, information is consumed by U.S. and foreign audiences at the same time via the same means.

To illustrate this fact, as this committee is aware, it was a 33-year-old IT [information technology] consultant in Abbottabad, Pakistan, that first reported the U.S. military raid against Osama bin Laden in 2011 on Twitter. This happened as events were still unfolding on the ground and hours before the American people were officially notified by the President of the United States address.

While the means and methods of communication have transformed significantly over the past decade, much of the U.S. Government thinking on shaping and responding in the information environment has remained largely unchanged, to include how we manage U.S. Government information dissemination and how we respond to the information of our adversaries. We are cognitively hamstrung for a myriad of reasons, to include lack of accountability and oversight, bureaucracy resulting in insufficient levels of resourcing, and inability to absorb cutting-edge information and analytic tools, and access to highly skilled personnel. This while our adversaries are increasing investment in the information environment, while not being constrained by ethics, the law, or even the truth.

The good news is that we have good people working this effort. The workforce is committed and passionate and recognize why this is important and why we as a nation need to get it right.

Again, thank you for the opportunity to be here, and I look forward to your questions.

[The prepared statement of Mr. Lumpkin can be found in the Appendix on page 50.]

Ms. STEFANIK. Thank you, Mr. Lumpkin.

I now recognize Mr. Thomas.

STATEMENT OF TIMOTHY L. THOMAS, SENIOR ANALYST, FOREIGN MILITARY STUDIES OFFICE, FORT LEAVENWORTH

Mr. THOMAS. Chairwoman Stefanik, distinguished members of the House Subcommittee on Emerging Threats and Capabilities, thank you for the opportunity to appear before you today to talk about Russian concepts and capabilities for information warfare.

By way of disclaimer, while I work for the Department of the Army as a senior analyst at the Foreign Military Studies Office, which does unclassified work, I am appearing today in my capacity as a subject matter expert and not as a person who can speak in an official capacity about Army or defense policy. As such, the views I express today are my own and do not necessarily reflect the views of the Department of the Army or Department of Defense.

Russia's information warfare approach is holistic. It is focused not only on media and propaganda, but on information technologies that fit weaponry as well. Ever since the 1990s, Russia has divided its information warfare concepts into two parts: Information technical and information psychological. Social media and cyber have tended to blend the two and caused a significant change in how Russia views the emerging trends in the character of warfare.

First, they note that nonmilitary activities, such as media use or information deterrence capabilities, are being used more often, they say by a ratio of four to one, than military ones.

And second, they note that information technologies reduce distance and make remote engagement, whether it be by international media, infiltration abroad, or the use of high-tech weapons to be considered as a principal tactic or means.

Forecasts are made after these trends are studied that reflect how conflict might unfold, which appears to be the general staff's development of a new type warfare scenario, the diagram of which was part of the written testimony. This new type warfare includes disorienting a victim state's leadership, creating dissatisfaction in the populace, intensifying diplomatic pressure and propaganda, applying cyber attacks and software effects, covertly deploying special forces, and using weapons based on either new physical principles, robotics, or other issues.

After trends and forecasts are made, a military strategy encompassing all aspects of military and state activity is established to take advantage of the forecast. An information strategy, according to one Russian source, is a state's use of information technologies and effects to attain information superiority over competitors in several areas. Evolving science and technology developments potentially alter the correlation of information-based forces along strategic sectors or in space.

Finally, forms and methods of employing the strategy are developed. The chief of the Russian General Staff Valery Gerasimov has stated often that the production of new forms and methods of warfare is an urgent task for military academies to develop. A form is an organization which in regard to information warfare could include international media elements such as Russia Today [RT] or Sputnik, or military developments, such as the creation of science companies or information operation forces.

These forms or organizations implement methods. Methods are composed of two parts: Weaponry and military art. Weaponry can include hackers, reflexive control techniques, trolls, disinformation, deterrence capabilities, and other agents of destruction or influence. Military art includes the use of indirect and asymmetric capabilities to achieve specific goals, such as the exploitation of the West's free press or an indirect attack on the cyber infrastructure of another nation. Russian's excellent contingent of algorithm writers ensures that the nation will be strong for years to come in writing software as weapons that could eavesdrop, persuade, or destroy.

To summarize, the effort is holistic, it follows trends, makes forecasts, strategies, and force correlations, and develops forms and methods to implement the strategy.

I thank you for your attention.

[The prepared statement of Mr. Thomas can be found in the Appendix on page 62.]

Ms. STEFANIK. Thank you, Mr. Thomas.

My question, I actually would like to start with you in regards to your testimony. When it comes to Russian propaganda and disinformation activities against NATO [North Atlantic Treaty Organization] and the EU [European Union], how damaging are their propaganda campaign against these organizations? And what impact is that having on U.S. national security and economic ties to Europe? And then the second part of my question is, knowing that I would like to focus on Russian propaganda dealing with NATO and the EU, can you also add another layer, you referenced the exploitation of the Western free press, how is that a part of their broader propaganda strategies?

Mr. THOMAS. Thank you. The first part of your question with regard to propaganda, propaganda is usually associated with emotional content. It varies from what you might call the disinformation aspect, which is designed to focus more on the logic of decision making. So what you will have as a combination of these two, the emotional aspect is aimed, I believe, more at the population of the country, whereas the disinformation aspect is aimed more at decision makers within the EU or NATO. The final goal would be, clearly, to disrupt or destroy the relationships among NATO and members of the EU.

The second part of your question which addressed Western thought and how Russia might take advantage of it, back in 1946, George Kennan noted that Russians do not believe in objective truth. If you fast forward ahead to about 2014, and you listen to some of their commentators, like Dmitry Kiselyov, Kiselyov noted that objectivity is a myth being imposed upon us. So what you have within the Russian information domain, if you want to call it that, is no real truth. You just have the ability to create an alternate reality, which doesn't coincide at all with the Western understanding of information in a free press.

Perhaps the best example of that was the downing of the Malaysia airliner. Immediately, we had our own understanding of what had happened. We had the intercepts. We had the images of the air defense platform leaving the area, yet for the next 3 or 4 years, we listened incessantly to Russian alternate views of what had happened, with the last one coming the day before the Netherlands released their report. They attempted to create an alternate reality.

This seems to be the focus of the propaganda effort there as they study us and they study audience behavior.

Thank you.

Ms. STEFANIK. I want to broaden my followup to Mr. Armstrong and Mr. Lumpkin. So what strategies do we need to pursue to counterbalance the example that Mr. Thomas just laid out?

Mr. LUMPKIN. I think we need to do—because we can develop strategies, we have to have a strategy for respective countries. One thing that I have learned in my time is that like all politics is local, all messaging is local as well. So a strategy that works for Russia, for example, countering their disinformation propaganda efforts, may or may not work in another nation, but each one has to be tailored. For example, if you were going to do counter-propaganda disinformation against Russia, you would want it to have a different strategy, for example, with Iran or any other nations that we were going to work with. And it is not just a nation-state issue; it is also true against violent extremist groups as well.

So I think the key is you have to understand the audience, have clear goals set out of what you want to achieve, and then develop a strategy that is unique to that particular audience.

Ms. STEFANIK. And that is something that Russia does, unfortunately, effectively. They have country-specific strategies when it comes to their disinformation and propaganda.

Mr. LUMPKIN. Absolutely. And I do believe that we have to think about information in the same way when you are going against other nation-states' efforts.

Ms. STEFANIK. Mr. Armstrong.

Mr. ARMSTRONG. So to add to Michael's comments, we need to understand the local information environment. I think one of the problems we suffer is that we mirror-image. We pretend that the local audiences know what we know, that they have the same access to the information, and that is simply often not the case. We have to pay attention that the Russians will make fake—not just deliver fake stories, whether it is a rape or some other abhorrent action to spur up local concerns and issues, but they will put fake experts on the air and they will create fake groups.

So it is one thing for us to come from the outside and probe into a country and say, this is what we need to say and what we need to do, but we need to help those nations and those markets, if you will, understand and be more critical about the information that they are getting.

One of the things that the Russians take advantage of is the lack of critical thinking. They don't want a critical thinker. A critical thinker is not the audience for a Russian media product. That is why they will throw out three or four, five, six, in the case of MH17, eight different stories lines at one time, maybe even within the same hour of broadcast, because it will resonate with different people in different ways. But they also have a tolerance for failure. So they will drop a story line if it is not working or they will drop an effort.

And that is one of the challenges that we have is that we have almost zero tolerance for failure. So we delay, we wait until we have it perfect, whereas our adversaries are spinning and trying and trying and trying until something actually works. So I would say we need to partner with local capacity and help develop local capacity.

Ms. STEFANIK. Thank you, Mr. Armstrong.

I now recognize Ms. Speier.

Ms. SPEIER. Thank you, Madam Chair. I want to thank you for having this hearing. I think this is really a critical area that we spend really too little time and underfund our efforts mightily.

I was struck when reading through the list of Russian military tactics for offensive media campaigns: Lies for the purposes of disinformation; focusing on the negative, which is more readily accepted than the positive; simplification, confirmation, and repetition; introducing taboos on categories of news. It sounds to me a lot like the 2016 Presidential campaign.

Now, don't get me wrong. I do firmly believe, based on all the available evidence, that Russia played a heavy hand as well, but as we have seen this behavior during the campaign continue in the Presidency, I am forced to wonder how much additional damage has been self-inflicted.

So, Mr. Thomas, would you assess that the undermining of public confidence in domestic and international institutions, attacks on the free press, are all consistent with Russian information warfare objectives?

Mr. THOMAS. Yes, I think that they are consistent. I think what you see when you listen to the Russians, is at home they have what I would call an echo chamber in that everything they say is being said by the same people over and over. The way they have tried to handle their audience vulnerabilities is they have stopped allowing surveys like we would have with a Gallup Poll so that they can limit vulnerabilities to that audience. Meanwhile, as Matt and Michael have said, they are studying the vulnerabilities in other countries to the best of their ability to find those—they look at the Gallup Polls and find where they might be able to place some important information.

Ms. SPEIER. So if you were to identify what our vulnerabilities are as seen by the Russians, what would they be?

Mr. THOMAS. I don't think I would be a person who could answer that particular question.

Ms. SPEIER. Do any of you have a comment on that? Mr. Armstrong.

Mr. ARMSTRONG. So I think it is really important. I think there are some good, obvious examples over in Europe right now. But with regard to the United States, I had a conversation with a senior Russian involved in their information activities, and they made a comment that there would not be a market in the United States for RT if the American media was doing their job. And I think there is some legitimacy to that, is that the polarization of our news has created some gaps and has—there is an interesting thing that RT has done, I believe. Where we perceive a linear spectrum, there is a far left and a far right, RT has managed to bend that so that they are addressing the far right and the far left simultaneously.

Now, they are generally on the fringes and it is easy for us to overestimate their impact, but their true impact, I think, is their seepage of their stories, of their messages, of their questioning that gets into our conversations. So I think that's where we should be looking at. But RT is not alone in that space.

Ms. SPEIER. So Mr. Clapper has suggested, as you pointed out in your testimony, re-creation of the USIA, although I guess one of you indicated not in its original form. I think that was you, Mr. Lumpkin. How would you see an agency that is robust in terms of putting out information in localities around the world, what would that look like to you?

Mr. LUMPKIN. Just to kind of follow up on my written statement is, I do believe that, based upon the complexity of the information environment, the numbers of actors and players within the U.S. Government, that there is a lot of people working hard, everybody's rowing the boat, not necessarily in the same direction. And I do believe that the creation of the GEC, the Global Engagement Center, was a step in the right direction on trying to coordinate, synchronize, and ultimately lead U.S. Government efforts.

Ms. SPEIER. But you said that, in the end, was suggestive.

Mr. LUMPKIN. Yes, and I believe that. Unfortunately, it is too mired in the bowels of the bureaucracy that it doesn't have the ability to direct the interagency nor advocate for resourcing. I believe if you elevated an entity to something similar to the Office of the Director of National Intelligence that could effectively coordinate and direct the interagency, you would be able to garner more resources, better synchronize the efforts, and have better end-states over U.S. information efforts against——

Ms. SPEIER. Okay. I have 15 seconds, and I have one more question for you, Mr. Lumpkin. Do you believe the hiring freeze is having a deleterious effect on our ability to respond?

Mr. LUMPKIN. I think it will. I do believe it will.

Ms. SPEIER. Thank you. I yield back.

Ms. STEFANIK. I now recognize Dr. Abraham.

Dr. ABRAHAM. Thank you, Madam Chair. And thank you for the very sobering testimony. I hope we and the Department of Defense take heed.

It appears that Russia and other state players are—have a lot of smoke and mirror-type technology where, unfortunately, we in America have to adhere just because of moralistic standards to a more rigid structure.

Mr. Lumpkin, you referenced a particular strategy for a particular state or a particular country. The problem is, as we all know, is that now there is a mixture and a menagerie of all these states and terrorist organizations that sometimes certainly cloud the picture. And I totally agree that, unfortunately, the way our laws and somewhat our citizenship, as far as being basic good people, we are restricted somewhat to being more of a reactionary than a proactive state. And I think we saw that in the OPM [Office of Personnel Management] breach.

The question I have is why has the USG been unable to unify and orient its various interested organizations and capabilities to compete in this broader information environment? What is the disconnect there?

Mr. LUMPKIN. I wish I could say that there was one thing that was the causal agent, but if we—I have had many jobs in my life. The most complicated and complex environment I ever operated in was being the special envoy and the coordinator at the Global Engagement Center, because the stakeholders are vast, budgets are all over the map, authorities are not aligned with the current environment between public affairs, information operations, and public diplomacy and—nor are the efforts. And I think it is, we are at the point where we need to take a step back, especially while technology in the world is continuing to advance and become more hyperconnected, to look at how we can effectively do this.

But I do believe we can have an overarching strategy in organization structure and then come up with substrategies for specific countries or groups.

Dr. ABRAHAM. So do you think maybe the DOD needs a global nonkinetic-type coordinator to kind of herd the cats?

Mr. LUMPKIN. Well, I don't know that it should be DOD that is leading the effort, and here is why: Because the information operations efforts are generally focused on title 10, support of military objectives.

Dr. ABRAHAM. Right.

Mr. LUMPKIN. And this is much larger than the military. They are a key stakeholder and a key component and probably the best resourced, but that doesn't mean that they should be leading the effort, because there are limitations to their authorities on how and where they can operate.

Dr. ABRAHAM. That is a little bit unsettling. The next question for you again, Mr. Lumpkin. And, Mr. Armstrong, please chime in, and Mr. Thomas, if you have comments.

What do you see as the major challenges for the Department of Defense today in conducting information operations and counterpropaganda within the structure that they now have?

Mr. LUMPKIN. I think that they continue to have resourcing challenges. Again, lots of good people working on this issue, just not enough of them. I think that is one part that they have got as far as people. There is the budget levels. As Mr. Armstrong mentions, there is also the tolerance for risk. We have to increase our acceptance of a risk and be able to iterate very rapidly when we do a— try to come up with a messaging program or strategy and we find it not effective, we have to iterate and move very rapidly. We have to build agility, which means that most of our work has to be underpinned with data analytics. It has to be an analytics-based structure, which means we have to have the analytic tools, capabilities, and access to talent that knows how to use them.

Dr. ABRAHAMS. And other state players, such as Russia, they don't even pay attention to the analytics; they just kind of throw them out of the window and say they really don't exist at all sometimes.

Mr. LUMPKIN. I am sure that is the case, but I would argue that because our adversaries have a very high threshold for risk, they can get it wrong a lot and still just inundate the airwaves and the information space.

Dr. ABRAHAMS. Anything to add, Mr. Armstrong, right quick?

Mr. ARMSTRONG. I do, thank you. So I would rephrase the same thing that Mr. Lumpkin said: There is an acceptance of a threat that is absent, there is a prioritization that is absent, and there is a strategy that is absent. So put another way, the combatant commander or the commander on the ground is going to be more concerned with LOAC, law of armed conflict, rather than the informational or psychological effect of an activity, which means in this transparent battlefield environment, the psychological effect of an action may be more narrow than what the legal—what the law allows. But yet they will have the lawyer there rather than the psyop or information officer there.

Dr. ABRAHAMS. Okay. Thank you.

Thank you, Madam Chair.

Ms. STEFANIK. Thank you.

I now recognize the ranking member, Mr. Langevin, for his opening statements and then the opportunity to ask questions.

STATEMENT OF HON. JAMES R. LANGEVIN, A REPRESENTATIVE FROM RHODE ISLAND, RANKING MEMBER, SUBCOMMITTEE ON EMERGING THREATS AND CAPABILITIES

Mr. LANGEVIN. Thank you, Madam Chair. And welcome to our witnesses here today. I apologize that I was late. My plane just landed a little while ago, and got here as quick as I could. But I am sorry I missed your opening statements, but we have your statements for the record, and I appreciate your being here today. So, Mr. Lumpkin, in particular, it is nice to see you again. Welcome back. And as the former Assistant Secretary of Defense for Special Operations and Low-Intensity Conflict as well as the prior special envoy of the Global Engagement Center at the Department of State, you certainly have valuable insight. I know that we have benefited, the government can benefit from his work to understand information operations conducted by our adversaries and improve U.S. efforts to counter propaganda and other activities under the IO umbrella.

Our other two witnesses, of course, also bring extraordinary perspectives. Mr. Armstrong was previously with the Broadcasting Board of Governors [BBG], and Mr. Thomas has spent his career in the IO fields and earned his expertise on Russia through extensive study. So I appreciate your perspectives and taking the time to be here today.

As the witnesses' robust backgrounds demonstrate, U.S. information operations require what I believe is a whole-of-government approach. This subcommittee has worked tirelessly on U.S. IO policy and capabilities over the years, and more recently focused on fine tuning our ability to counter propaganda. One such effort is a provision in the National Defense Authorization Act for Fiscal Year 2017 that expands the scope of the Global Engagement Center to include countering propaganda of nation-state actors, which is the focus of today's hearing.

Nation-states, like the Russian Federation, use the information environment outside of a combat zone in a strategic effort to intimidate, to undermine, and control allies, as well as stymie U.S. objectives. They are doing so in an increasingly aggressive and overt manner as evidenced by Russia's recent acknowledgment of the formation of new IO troops.

IO is only one component of Russia's strategy to achieve objectives, but their tactics, their techniques and procedures often executed with complete disregard for international norms have proven effective at achieving favorable conditions for their underlying intentions and their motivations.

The United States is not a nation that will disregard the law or compromise basic values. Data collection, analysis, and storage required to inform our own counter-propaganda and information operations writ large, especially outside the combat zone and using social media, must continue to comply with domestic and international law. The United States overt messaging must always be delivered consistently and maintain a truth and integrity.

In accordance with our values, we must improve the U.S. Government and our allies' ability to counter IO of other actors and take back the narrative in order to promulgate truth. This effort will require us to ask hard questions, such as, is the government organized for and prioritizing effective IO? Is the Department of State force structure which—I am sorry. Is the Department of Defense force structure, which currently aligns IO capabilities to many commands, conducive to effective employment of information operations in concert with other interagency efforts outside of an area of active hostilities?

The U.S. must leverage technological advancements and other new capabilities in a timely manner. The Department of Defense must also be able to effectively employ such capabilities with operational funding authorities that allow for flexibility in an ever-evolving information environment while still maintaining transparency and oversight of activities.

Finally, and most importantly, U.S. strategies and military commander objectives for addressing threats must be realistic and holistic. We must leverage all tools at our disposal for disruption, deterrence, and response, while mitigating conflict escalation in the development of ever more pernicious techniques for conducting influence campaigns.

So with that, I will stop there and go to questions.

Ms. STEFANIK. Yes.

Mr. LANGEVIN. Okay. So again, thanks to our witnesses.

Mr. Lumpkin, if I could, based on your experience in the DOD, what role should Cyber Command [CYBERCOM] have in countering IO of nation-state military or nonmilitary actors outside of an area of hostilities? And does that change if the IO is being conducted on U.S. soil? And is there more that can be done to leverage the capabilities of this command consistent with international and other laws?

Mr. LUMPKIN. I believe that CYBERCOM is a key player in this space. When you look at—and this is why in the language of the 2017 National Defense Authorization Act it was critical that it said countering—to go against—counter-state propaganda and disinformation efforts. It allowed us to think differently about the problem set, to look at this—this isn't a tit for tat in the information space, but rather looking at the entire tools of government that can be applied against this problem set. And I think CYBERCOM is a key player in this space.

Now, I do recognize and appreciate the lines of authority of operating domestically for CYBERCOM, and I respect those lines. But that said, it is becoming much more difficult to see where information starts and where it stops. It is very difficult to see whether somebody is an American citizen when they are using a computer in a nation outside of the United States. There is no passport with an IP [internet protocol] address. So as we look to what affects U.S. citizens and what affects domestic policy, the lines are very gray and very blurred right now.

Mr. LANGEVIN. Thank you.

Mr. Thomas, you stress in your testimony that Russia perceives it is under attack from the West. If the U.S. ramps up its own IO and other efforts to counter their indirect warfare activities, how do we do so in a manner that decreases the risk of conflict escalation and modern warfare arms race?

Mr. THOMAS. Well, the first—the very first thing that I would be thinking of is for us to counter what Russia is doing, you really have to understand what they are doing. And what I mean by that is the tools that they have, the tools they use are different than some other nations, specifically because of their ability to use half truths or lies and get away with it, because they have, as we have said, an echo chamber that everybody's kind of on the same page when you listen to the evening news. But you have to understand what they mean when they say, I am employing information deter- rence, when they say I am employing reflexive control, when I am using trolls. People really have to understand the lay of the land. Probably the best issue you can think of is if two teams are play- ing basketball and— we are into the Final Four here of March Mad- ness—one team is not practicing against its own offense in practice. It is practicing against what the other guy is set up for offense and what kind of defense they play. And it is kind of the same way with looking at Russian propaganda and disinformation activities. You have to understand what it is objectively that sits behind the way they do business. It is different than us. And once that is un- derstood, you have a base from which you can then begin to re- spond. Thank you.

Mr. LANGEVIN. Thank you.

Okay. And to all of our witnesses, in your opinion, what are the most effective capabilities and activities the U.S. can employ to deter, disrupt, and counter IO of nation-states, specifically propa- ganda, for deterrence and disruption? Is it disruption or denial of service to our adversary or dissemination of truthful narrative or are sanctions outside of the IO space most effective, for example, sanctions?

Mr. ARMSTRONG. So if—before I answer that question, if I can go back to your previous question to Mr. Thomas. I think there is a challenge here that we must not be accepting the Russian nar- rative, that they say that they are perceiving being attacked by the West is part of Putin's game. So I think part of the problem is we are too quick to accept their narrative and to undermine that nar- rative. He is riding a tiger that he has to keep finding an outside target for everybody.

And that leads into the answer to your question. I think that you gave several options, and I think the answer is yes, it depends on the situation. There is certainly an issue that we have with regard to Russia, as well as China, as reciprocity. We permit Russian media to operate here freely just as we would because that is our principles, those are our principles, and we allow Chinese media to operate freely. However, both countries deny our access, either our commercial media or our government media. For example, the BBG, for Voice of America [VOA], Radio Free Europe, are denied access to Russia, and China denies VOA and Radio Free Asia.

So I think there is an issue of reciprocity, but I also think there are elements where there needs to be, if you will, a more cyber— or rather a more physical type of attack response to their various activities. This is an incursion, it is a digital incursion, but I think there are times where a similar response is needed, just as much we need to get our message out there and make our statements. So the answer would be yes to all.

Mr. LANGEVIN. Okay.

Mr. LUMPKIN. I agree that all of those are very important and need to be an area of focus. I would add one more, if I could. It would be leveraging our partners. We have many partners who see the Russian threat in particular as existential, as something they live with every day.

Last year, I was in Lithuania and had some opportunity to talk to people and to get to understand the problem set and how they see the world. They have some very talented people who, frankly, there are many folks that are just looking for a little leadership. And I think it is one of the things we can do is to work with our partners to make sure we help build their capabilities, because this is a problem much bigger than just with us here in the United States. But I think we can leverage and lean heavily on our allies to carry a lot of water for us.

Mr. LANGEVIN. Agreed, agreed. Thank you. Well said. All of you, thank you very much.

I yield back.

Ms. STEFANIK. Mr. Scott.

Mr. SCOTT. Thank you, Madam Chair.

And, Mr. Armstrong, you talked about a lot of the issues that I had written down, state-owned media versus free press, that 24-hour-a-day, 7-day-a-week news cycle where sensationalizing and getting it fast is more important to the news channels than getting it right. I can't name a journalist anymore, to be honest with you. I think that is a greater threat to our country than any outside influence.

But with regard to this type of warfare, if you will, it is the exact opposite from a strategy standpoint as traditional war from what I can tell. I mean, we have always had—a country's capabilities were typically limited by their capacity. Capacity could be money, it could be the ability to get food and ammo to your soldiers, it could be manpower. Geography in and of itself limits a country's capacities. We are talking about Russia. You know, I don't think Russia has the ability to carry out operations in the Ukraine, Poland, the Baltic States, Syria. I don't think their economy allows them to do that right now. But their economy does allow them to create chaos, and then wherever they see the weakest point or the cheapest opportunity, if you will, to take advantage of it.

And so I have two questions, specifically with offense is cheap in this type of warfare and defense is expensive. So with that said, how do you limit the capacity of your adversary if you are not playing offense? And then two is, do you think that Russia has an endgame in mind or do you think that their goal is to create chaos and then simply take advantage of whatever weak points they see?

Mr. ARMSTRONG. Thank you for that question. Starting with your second question, yes. I think they have an endgame, and I think you answered that. I think it is the chaos to allow them—they would prefer to set up bilateral relations. They would prefer their adversaries or the other nations, Europe, not just us, to be in turmoil so that they can seed any message they want in there and they can get whatever they want to achieve out.

As far as what is a good defense to an aggressive offense, I think this is something where a good offense is a good defense. We are—as I said in my testimony, we are on our back feet. We are on our heels. We are responsive and reactive. And as the comment I made earlier about the Russian media leader, we are creating all sorts of opportunities for them. We don't have a strategy. As I said in my testimony, we have a credibility gap, and that creates not just a domestic vulnerability but a foreign vulnerability. When we don't have—this has been going on for years. When we don't have a clear, concise strategy and our adversaries are able to exploit that or when they manufacture a gap and we are unable to defend that and close that gap by exposing the truth, it is a vulnerability.

So I would go back to my earlier comment that we need to understand that this is a priority. This is asymmetric warfare. This is on the cheap. It is an ability to gain your foreign policy objectives very easily. As the chairwoman said in her opening statement, that this is the ability to reach into another nation very freely, very easily. So I think we need to prioritize this and we need to understand that this is a risk. And we can't, as Mr. Lumpkin said, we cannot separate cyber data, as I would call it, and cyber psychological. This is a merged environment.

Mr. SCOTT. So the only way to limit their capacity is for us to be on offense, not defense?

Mr. ARMSTRONG. Well, yes. And I would add, undercut their will to act in that way.

Mr. SCOTT. Fair enough.

Mr. ARMSTRONG. If they don't perceive value, there is no risk, there is no cost. So I think part of this too is our lack of strategy is we have not established an escalation ladder. We don't necessarily need to publish that because somebody will come right up to it, as they are in hybrid warfare.

Mr. SCOTT. Someone may publish it for us.

Mr. ARMSTRONG. But we don't know when it is too much. We haven't decided that. So we don't know when we are going to react. And I think the Russians are a perfect example of a group that is willing to keep literally and virtually pushing——

Mr. SCOTT. I am down to 20 seconds. Would you agree then that they are not going to stop until we stop them?

Mr. ARMSTRONG. Agree completely.

Mr. SCOTT. Thank you very much.

Gentlemen, thank you for your service to the country.

Ms. STEFANIK. Mrs. Murphy.

Mrs. MURPHY. Thank you all for being here.

Mr. Lumpkin, you were recently leading the Global Engagement Center at the State Department, an organization that was created last year to lead and coordinate the Federal Government's counter-propaganda efforts. In your written testimony and as you have discussed a bit here today, you suggest that the center should be elevated above the assistant secretary level at State in order to give the organization more authority to direct the interagency.

What sort of resources and authorities would it take to elevate the center to something akin to the Office of the Director of National Intelligence? And do you have examples of how the current interagency structure prevents us from having an effective governmentwide information warfare and counter-propaganda strategy?

Mr. LUMPKIN. First, I think, let me take the second part of that first. What I found as the special envoy and coordinator for Global Engagement Center, I had so many peers, so my position was relegated to suggesting action. I had no influence over budgets, how they spent their money, where they put their people, and what was a priority and what was not. In order for me to—I had a very good working relationship and we were able to do a lot based on power of personality, and based on me coming directly from the Department of Defense previously. But there are a host of different players in this. You have got USAID [United States Agency for International Development], the regional bureaus at the State Department, you have got the intelligence community [IC], you have CYBERCOM, you have many different organizations that have a role here to play. And it is just trying to herd those cats to get them to actually do what you need to do. That is the problem set as far as organization.

Again, using my analogy, is everybody is rowing the boat really hard, just not necessarily in the same direction, which impedes forward progress.

I do believe there are several ways this could be done. I think it is best done through legislation, just as what was done with the GEC being codified and expanding its mission set to include the counter-state and disinformation efforts. I think that is generally the best mechanism to get things changed to be enduring. So that would be my first—and also make sure everybody's got skin in the game, which I think is important from a resourcing perspective, and not just leaving it up to the executive branch to sort this out, because we all own this problem set.

Mrs. MURPHY. And then my second question is about our efforts to counter ISIL [Islamic State of Iraq and the Levant] propaganda on the internet and to make it harder for them to recruit online. To be successful, this effort requires U.S. personnel, military and civilian, with the proper linguistic skills as well as cultural skills to be able to understand what they are reading and engage.

A recent article about the CENTCOM [Central Command] program to counter ISIL's online propaganda indicated that our efforts may not be effective or at least as effective as they could be. I raised this issue at a previous hearing with Michael Sheehan, who ran NYPD's [New York Police Department's] counterterrorism operations. Mr. Sheehan said that the Federal security clearance process is the real obstacle, which makes it hard for qualified linguists to get cleared to do this critical work for the Federal Government. He noted that at NYPD, they put their linguists in a box, as he put it, so that they could do their work without having access to classified information. He suggested the NYPD model could be replicated on the Federal level. Would you comment on this idea?

Mr. LUMPKIN. I think there is some merit to it. One of the authorities that was granted to the Global Engagement Center was access—it is leveraging what they call section 3161, which is a hiring authority, which allowed the GEC to hire people to work in the U.S. Government uncompetitively based on their skill sets for a limited term.

For example, it gave me access to folks in Silicon Valley, Madison Avenue, people who were pros in this space, in addition to folks who have unique cultural or language capabilities that I could—the challenge I always ran into is the security clearance requirement, because what I found within the Department of State, it takes about the same time to get somebody a top secret access to sensitive compartmented intelligence as it does a confidential clearance.

So normally it takes about, I am told, a year to 18 months. What I was able to do is, one individual, we were able to fast track it, we put a lot of pressure on the system, and we did it in 5 months. I know it can be done, but that was a one-off. It doesn't happen every time.

Mrs. MURPHY. And do you think that there is a way to hire some of these people and box them in such that they don't need a clearance?

Mr. LUMPKIN. I think it depends on—I think it can be done. It is problematic, especially if you are looking in collaborative work environments, where—an information space that is very dynamic and is moving in real time. It is very hard to go out to a box and get somebody's—it is difficult.

So, I mean, it is a short-term solution, but it will have long-term consequences of not being as productive as it could be. A better option would be to find ways to fast track the security clearance process to bring the right people in to do the mission set that needs to be done.

Mrs. MURPHY. Great. Thank you.

Ms. STEFANIK. Mr. Franks.

Mr. FRANKS. Well, thank you, Madam Chair.

And thank you, gentlemen, for being here.

You know, I think there is consensus that on the tactical level America has very effectively engaged the terrorist groups throughout the world. We win the battle on the battlefield, but we really haven't engaged them on the strategic level as effectively as we should, namely their narrative of global jihad.

And I guess my first question is related to the Global Engagement Center. Do you believe that we need to encourage or to make sure that the GEC places a greater emphasis on Islamist theology and jihadist ideology if it is to effectively counter the propaganda success of jihadi groups like ISIS, or is the problem just a lack of money?

Mr. LUMPKIN. Well——

Mr. FRANKS. Mr. Lumpkin, yes, sir——

Mr. LUMPKIN. Yeah, no, I have looked at this problem set quite a bit. And as I look at ISIS, if I look at ISIS and I see how they recruit and who they recruit, when they are recruiting from abroad, they are generally going after vulnerable populations.

The way I kind of do the math, is there is about 7 billion, 7.5 billion people on the planet, okay. At the height of ISIS, there was about 30,000 of them, 30,000 people. We know how many people have been killed, how many people have been wounded, and how many people have defected from the battlefield, plus or minus, which leads us to a number between 9,000 and 19,000 that joined this organization per year.

When I simplify it like that and I look at—so we have 7.5 billion people being held hostage by 9,000 to 19,000 recruits every year. In order to find those people, we have to use scalpel-like messages that resonate with those individuals instead of just going after one broad of a—Islamic messages, because people join ISIS for different reasons.

The best study I have seen was done by the group called Quantum out of Lebanon, which basically binned those people who joined ISIS into nine different bins, everything from death seekers to thrill seekers, some are hardcore fundamentalists, some are looking for redemption. But each one of those groups, when you understand the recruit and you understand the audience, you have to target why they joined, and you have to come up with messaging strategies against each and every one of those groups.

Mr. FRANKS. So do you believe that the challenge is just a lack of funding or more specifically focusing on those messages that you have cited?

Mr. LUMPKIN. I think you have challenges in both. I will tell you, in 2015, we—the U.S. Government, did a single kinetic strike against a high-value target that cost the U.S. taxpayers—when you look at the intelligence gathering before and after the strike was about $250 million that had about 2 weeks of difference of impact on the battlefield to take out one high-value target.

That same year in messaging, we spent about $5.6 million in base funding. So we have a discrepancy in where we want to put our money. Because I will tell you, I can tell you what your priorities are based on where you put your money and where you put your people. And in 2015, we weren't resourced appropriately. We have made huge strides in a short amount of time, but we still have a ways to go.

Mr. FRANKS. All right. Well, let me shift gears on you here just a little bit.

To combat the Russian hybrid warfare, do we merely need to park armored brigade combat teams in Eastern Europe without improving our cyber capabilities or hardening our space assets, in order to deter Russia, or do we have to sort of have a mirror effort to be able to engage them at and oppose them at every stage of their hybrid warfare?

And that would be Mr. Thomas, I think.

Mr. THOMAS. Congressman, first of all, this is just my own personal opinion. I don't think Russia does hybrid war. I know a lot of people think they do.

What we see when we read their press, initially they were doing something called new generation war, and that had to do a lot with initially pressuring the leaders and then gradually working into a regular warfare-type scenario where they deployed special forces and then they had more traditional combat.

That term went away in 2013 and has been replaced by the diagram that I put in the testimony of new type warfare. I think why it is important is because that diagram enables you to see a scenario finally, a template of how Russia does envision what a future war might look like.

I certainly understand why many people still ascribe Russian efforts as hybrid, because they, from our definition, it appears that way. But as we study them, we tend to look at the Russian version because that is our job, you know, we look at what they write all the time. But ever since that moment in 2013 or 2015 when this template was proposed, they have been using that and the guys who talk new generation now talk new type as well.

So what have they done that would answer your question, they tend to—as you know, in this coming year they are going to have a big exercise in the western district. They have increased their— the number of divisions there; in other words, they have increased the correlation of forces there with three new divisions.

I think that General Hodges and others in Europe are doing what they can to offer a counter, let them know that if they did try to provoke actions or if they did try to come across the border, there would be a deterrent to that activity.

So I think what we are doing at the moment is absolutely what is needed. The question becomes when can both sides start to pull back, you know, when can we talk about equal security where we both feel secure. And like Michael said, how do we get them out of this feeling of this existential situation where everybody, on both the Baltic side, they feel like they are being—their survival is under threat and the Russians basically feel the same way.

Mr. FRANKS. Thank you, Madam Chair.

Thank you, gentlemen.

Ms. STEFANIK. Mr. Cooper.

Mr. COOPER. Thank you, Madam Chair, for an excellent hearing, and thank the witnesses.

Mr. Armstrong, you had mentioned in your answer to, I think, Ms. Speier's question that there are other RTs operating in the U.S. Can you describe them, list them?

Mr. ARMSTRONG. Sure. Thank you.

So you have RT, you have Sputnik, you have Ruptly, and then I think you have them feeding other entities, Infowars comes to mind, where those are echo chambers for those modalities. I would suspect that you have a variety of other groups. There was a project I was looking at with some colleagues. We were looking at VK, VKontakte, the social media site, the Russian social media site where American white supremacists were flocking to VK because social media sites in the U.S., like Facebook, were kicking them off.

And what we found was, it appeared that American white supremacists were happily involved in discussions there, and there were very Russian, not cloaked but Russian actors in those spaces as well. So I think this is another insidious way of spinning or getting into the conversation. So I think besides these larger organizations, there is a lot of stuff that they are doing on the margins.

Mr. COOPER. Are Chinese efforts in any way comparable to this?

Mr. ARMSTRONG. I think the Chinese are more sophisticated. RT is willing to play on the margins and play at the extremes, and China is a much more sophisticated actor. They are—I think if you want to compare which one lies more, which one distorts the truth more, I think RT's slogan of "question more" fits them because they don't want you to find an answer. They just want you to be confused.

And CCTV is a much more intellectual and they are trying to push the Chinese view, but I think they do tend to be a more professional operation. So I wouldn't equate them, per se, on the same level. I don't think that either of them are particularly good for the American market.

Mr. COOPER. Mr. Thomas, I appreciated your detailed knowledge of Russian techniques, particularly reflexive control. I think you quoted Kennan as saying that the Russians don't believe in objective truth. Was that from the Long Telegram or some other of Kennan's writings? Do you remember?

Mr. THOMAS. Yes, it was.

Mr. COOPER. How many other countries do you think have leaders that share a similar philosophy of not believing in objective truth, whether they articulate that or not?

Mr. THOMAS. Uh-huh. Well, I do think that that is probably the situation in China as well because they are strongly Marxist as well, and anytime that you look at what is being taught in the schools, especially in the propaganda schools, they are looking, first of all, at how do I visualize objective reality, and then subjectively, how do I manipulate those factors to my benefit. That basically is their definition of strategy, by the way. So we do see that.

One other thing I could add to what Matt said is that when you look at Chinese propaganda in the United States, it is interesting that you do see a subtler aspect like Sun Tzu institutes where language is being taught in 39 or so universities.

And you also see—I remember the last time I stayed at a hotel here in Washington. There were two newspapers offered to me in the morning, the Washington Post and the China Daily. And when you start to see that, you realize that there—in one of the books I wrote the Chinese did say point-blank that they needed to take over the cultural environment in other countries. And so there is an effort underway, with CCTV and others, to more gradually, I think, than the Russian version, which is quite dramatic and offensive.

Mr. COOPER. I don't know if any of you gentlemen have seen the movie "Occupied." It is a 10-part European series about the takeover of Norway by Russia on energy issues. It was very subtly done. I find when I am explaining defense policy to folks back home, it is easier if I refer to a movie they might have seen because they tend to have such disbelief and they don't read newspapers.

So any popular materials you could suggest to us that might help average people understand would be very useful. Thank you.

Thank you, Madam Chair.

Ms. STEFANIK. Thank you, Mr. Cooper.

We will now go to the second round of questions for those members who want another opportunity.

My question, I will start with Mr. Lumpkin. Some have advocated for the creation of a U.S. Information Agency 2.0, bringing together the technical capabilities of cyber with some of the traditional information and communications component. Is that something that GEC, the Global Engagement Center, can build into? What is your opinion on that, having headed the Global Engagement Center, on whether that is a viable proposal?

Mr. LUMPKIN. I think that there is merit to a USIA, U.S. Information Agency-like organization. I am loathe for more bureaucracy. So what I would like to do is to envision something that is more above the bureaucracy that can leverage what is already happening in government and get it to work better together and to make sure it is fully resourced, both in moneys and people.

But I do believe that we have significant capability in the U.S. Government; we just have to harness it, and, again, do that without creating too much bureaucratic tension or significant expense.

Ms. STEFANIK. And just to delve a little bit further into that, harnessing the capabilities we have today, can you talk about specific steps we can take to continue to mature the Global Engagement Center or continue to provide the resourcing that is necessary; and then the third piece is making sure that there is interagency communication rather than interagency friction.

Mr. LUMPKIN. I think you can do that by elevating the Global Engagement Center within the Federal Government and increase its authority by doing so. I think that will do that. I do believe that there are several other things that can be done. I think having access to key talent, the 3161 hiring authority, which is only through the executive order, so if that executive order were to go away, the 3161 hiring authority would go away as well.

So—and that authority, because the executive order was only for the countering violent extremist mission set, the interpretation is that it can only be used for that mission set. So you cannot use the 3161 hiring authority for the counter-state and disinformation efforts mission set within the Global Engagement Center.

So I think those are some key things that can be done. The other thing of significance is the GEC does not have a dedicated budget line. So it was funded largely through public diplomacy dollars, but it was up to the discretion of the senior leadership at the State Department on what that budget line would be from year to year. And there is a lack of stability in that funding, so it is hard to make long-term decisions, and it is also difficult to use that color of money, that type of money, that public diplomacy money to build partner capacity, to teach our partners and make our partners effective in this space. Because the more they do, the less we have to.

Ms. STEFANIK. Mr. Armstrong or Mr. Thomas, do you have comments on that line of questioning?

Mr. ARMSTRONG. I do. Thank you.

The notion of a new USIA I found very difficult to stomach, because as I have written about, USIA was created as a part two of a two-part reorganization of government by Eisenhower. And unless we are going to reorganize government, it is going to be really difficult to just recreate this thing because it was a simpler communication environment. It was also a simpler government. We have a much more complex space.

I would echo Mr. Lumpkin's comments, but I would also add that we are ignoring that there is an office in the State Department now that I think GEC, in some ways, and its predecessor CSCC [Center for Strategic Counterterrorism Communications], was trying to not just augment but in a way bypass or replace, and that is the Office of the Under Secretary of Public Diplomacy and its operation the Bureau of International Information Programs, which is the true legacy of United States Information Agency in that it was a global information center.

It does not have the flexibility either because of authority or leadership to do these things, and so CSCC was stood up and I think this recent GEC amendment, which originally took shape as the Portman-Murphy amendment, which was intentionally bypassing R, the Under Secretary for Public Diplomacy, I think it should be a wakeup call that R is not executing within the Department, it is marginalized within the Department. It is not executing what you need as far as foreign policy and national security.

And as Mr. Lumpkin just said, even the money within there and with the—both the authorities and the leadership, it has been a challenge to properly support GEC.

And what is interesting, and this goes into what Ranking Member Langevin started to—accidentally started to say "State force structure," I think there is a need to dramatically review the State Department's force structure along these lines, because one of the realities is that State Department has forward presence everywhere, everywhere. They have local expertise everywhere, and they are dramatically underfunded, undersupported. They are not experiencing these type of hearings. They don't have the same oversight. And, you know, they are out there on the ground utterly underfunded, undersupported, and not trained.

I would like to add too, is that while the Russians are training their foreign service in—we can call it next generation warfare or we can call it hybrid warfare, but they are training their foreign service in this regard.

And I met with some of their version of FSI [Foreign Service Institute], MGIMO [Moscow State Institute of International Relations], and they were citing Frank Hoffman, one of our military writers on this, and they were wondering why Frank is so militaristic. But this is their civilian side, and we have no comparable support to our foreign service or our foreign ministry.

Ms. STEFANIK. Thank you.

Mr. Langevin.

Mr. LANGEVIN. Thank you. That was an interesting perspective. And on that, I would ask Mr. Lumpkin if he had anything to add to what Mr. Armstrong just had to say about the State Department?

Mr. LUMPKIN. I only have 1 year of experience at the State Department, so my perspective is probably not—it is not as robust as my time in the Department of Defense. That said, people who know me know that I am not a huge fan of bureaucracy. I am not. I appreciate the need for it to standardize routine tasks.

I had thought I had seen bureaucracy at the Department of Defense until I got to the State Department. It is much thicker, much more ingrained. Wicked smart people, amazingly smart people, but I affectionately refer to the State Department as a 19th century bureaucracy using 20th century tools against a 21st century adversary. And we have to do better.

Mr. LANGEVIN. Thank you.

This is a question for all of our witnesses: How can we better leverage technological advancements to counter IO activities of other nations? Specifically, how can the U.S., particularly the Department of Defense, spur innovation and obtain new technological capabilities?

Mr. LUMPKIN. I would like to take that one. There is a lot of—especially in the world of analytics, there are tremendous number of tools. Last time I looked, there was between 3,400 and 3,800 analytic tools just on social media alone. It is an area of technology and science that is emerging every day, that is continuing to advance and to iterate itself.

What we have to do is to find ways to streamline access to those tools so we can get them put on U.S. Government systems. We are talking information technology systems, computer software, to get those implemented. So we need to fast track or streamline access to those because they are changing so fast.

And the social media environment and the media environment writ large is changing so rapidly, what we find ourselves frequently doing is putting 2-year-old tools into the workforce because that is how long it takes to get approvals to use them in many cases. So we have to find and streamline to keep up with technological advancements and leverage those things that can make our workforce more productive, more effective, and so we can speed our messaging capabilities.

Mr. ARMSTRONG. Can I add to that. I would say, one, we have to understand what we want to achieve. I think simply "stop it" is inadequate. I think we need to have a broader strategy, and I think we need to have a cost. We need to impose a cost on them to continue to conduct these activities, and I don't see that that is part of our process.

Mr. THOMAS. If I might add just one or two things quickly. Russia has developed what they call science companies. They have got about 10 or 11 of them now within the military. Those science companies unite new, young brains with the older guys, and they are learning from one another about electronic warfare and programming and these sort of things.

They also have an advanced research foundation, which is—they have created. It is similar to DARPA [Defense Advanced Research Projects Agency]. But they are into all of the things that DARPA is and robotics and UAVs [unmanned aerial vehicles] and all of these type of issues as well.

And perhaps most important of all has been the Russian education system. They continue to churn out incredible mathematicians and algorithm writers. And as anyone knows, you know, the key to software is in search engines, is algorithms and what it produces. And those are the—there is a high-tech capability there that they have invested in for sure.

Thank you.

Mr. LANGEVIN. Sure. I don't disagree with that at all. Point well taken.

So this is more of a longer term issue, well short and long term. But to all witnesses, so the U.S. has struggled with gauging the effectiveness of our own messaging and other IO efforts. In your opinion, how can we improve U.S. ability to measure effectiveness of IO activities and overall impact of operations?

Mr. LUMPKIN. This goes back to the analytic tools I was talking about, is to making sure we have access to them and also make sure that any strategies we develop and as we move forward especially in the counter-state propaganda and disinformation space is that they have to be underpinned with analytics.

And it is not just assessing whether your message is effective; if it is not, is how are you going to change it rapidly, reassessed and—and change and change. Because at the speed of information it has to constantly be iterated for the consumer to keep up with the 24-hour, 7-days-a-week, 365-days-a-year news and information cycle that is out there.

So I think the data is key to both what we do every day and how you stay relevant in this space.

Mr. LANGEVIN. Thank you.

Ms. STEFANIK. Mr. Cooper.

Mr. COOPER. Thank you.

I would like to explore for a second the extent to which your worlds intersect with liberal arts academics in this country. Like, there are lots of theories on social cohesion, social capital, trust in the society, things like that. The work of Robert Putnam or anybody like that mean anything to you guys, or is that just——

Mr. LUMPKIN. I think one of the keys for the Global Engagement Center is there is several academic affiliations where you look at—because this is about behavior, right, when it is all said and done. It is about creating cognitive realities for people, whether it is based on logic or it is based on emotion, to change their ultimate behavior. So the behavior aspects of this are pretty much everything when it is said and done.

Mr. COOPER. That is why I am asking the question. He is more on the sociology side. On the behavioral economics side there are folks like Daniel Kahneman, won the Nobel Prize. There are theorists like Jonathan Haidt wrote the "Righteous Mind: Why Good People Fight Over Politics and Religion." Do you intersect with these worlds at all?

Mr. LUMPKIN. The GEC does, absolutely, and myself as a recovering anthropologist before I actually joined the United States Navy many years ago, so I have a deep-seated appreciation for the impacts of anthropology, sociology, and the other liberal arts, and the effects of what we are trying to actually do, so yes.

Mr. COOPER. So it's true that you can't conduct a public opinion poll in Russia or presumably in China? Is that right?

Mr. ARMSTRONG. So because they are difficult spaces to get into, there is one—I think there were two, but there was one, Levada, which was essentially the well-known Russian independent public opinion center. If memory serves, there was something that happened that caused relatively recently that they are no longer viewed that way, because—so it is difficult to do surveys in Russia. And China, I am not sure what our capacity is.

Mr. COOPER. It seems like an environment in which there is no trusted source, and that seems to be increasingly true in this country, like I spoke at Rotary in Nashville this Monday, and I have said that, well, 17 U.S. intelligence agencies agreed there was some sort of Russian involvement in our election. We don't know the extent or whether anybody was persuaded, but at least they tried. And I got a lot of pushback from Rotarians who said, well, why do you believe those guys. Like shouldn't unanimity among 17 U.S. intelligence agencies mean something to the average patriotic citizen?

Mr. ARMSTRONG. So going to your earlier question, I think there is a marketplace for loyalty that is evolving here, and there is a redefinition of citizenship and national security and nationalism, of who do you trust? Where is your alignment? In that particular situation, what I am about to say doesn't apply, but in the broader sense, you can now test drive another identity.

This goes into your behavioral concepts. You can now test drive an identity, and nobody has to know about it. You can reconnect with a vast culture that you have no connection. As I mentioned in the opening remarks about Jihad Jane, you can have no affiliation, ethnic, cultural, linguistic and decide you want to be part of something.

So there is an element here that is evolving our notion of hyphenates to commas where you can carry multiple identities at once. And from a marketing perspective, each one of those is an opportunity for me to subvert you and do something.

So I think that there is a challenge here that is playing within our trust scheme as well, even if it is not an outside actor, but who do we trust. I think this goes into the polarization of news. So we are continuing to subdivide, and I see nothing that is moving to reverse that pathway right now.

Mr. COOPER. In the newspaper today, they say that the German Government is considering imposing a 50,000 euro fine or something for fake news on the German internet. Do you know of any country that has done something like that?

Mr. ARMSTRONG. Well, one, each nation has a different relationship to the news. Our—such an act in our society would be very, very difficult. There is a comparable—each of the Baltic States, I think, have similar. They have tried—was it Estonia? No, it was Latvia that actually shut down Russian TV, and they continued to make efforts like that.

Britain has Ofcom, which is their regulatory for TV broadcast. They recently shut down RT's London U.K. bank account under those regulations. Now, that just covers broadcast so it doesn't cover internet.

So each nation has a different relationship to what news is flowing within their environment, so the answer is, yes, it does pose interesting challenges in various places because it can become a propaganda coup against that state.

Mr. COOPER. Thank you, Madam Chair. I see I have used my time. Thanks.

Ms. STEFANIK. Ms. Speier.

Ms. SPEIER. We just got word that the President has recommended a 28 percent cut in the State Department.

Mr. COOPER. Thirty seven percent.

Ms. SPEIER. Well, I heard 28, but—and I think there is a belief by some that by cutting that and cutting foreign aid that we are somehow not impacting our national security. And I think, Mr. Thomas, you had commented earlier, and I would like you to explore for us the impacts on national security, cuts to foreign aid and information distribution in foreign countries, as anemic as it is for us, how that will affect our national security.

Mr. THOMAS. Congresswoman, I don't think I can answer that question properly. I think I would rather defer to a State Department person.

Ms. SPEIER. All right. Mr. Lumpkin.

Mr. LUMPKIN. I think a cut of that magnitude would have devastating consequences on everything from the goodness that the State Department does from Fulbright scholarships that help, you know, bring people and access people and bring the world closer together and have people understand who we are as a nation and what our values are and what we believe.

I know that on—I just look at, from my time at DOD in conjunction with the State Department, we are not going to kill our way to victory. We are not going to message our way to victory. This is about having a layered approach to what we do, and you cannot cut—make a 37 percent cut to a single department that has such a crucial role without having devastating consequences.

Ms. SPEIER. Mr. Armstrong.

Mr. ARMSTRONG. So I think, like Mr. Lumpkin, we would both say that the State Department is a dysfunctional place and full of bureaucracy. That said, it needs to be revamped rather than massive cuts. Even elements such as exchanges, they historically have been part of the United States Government's efforts to win or engage in the struggle for minds and wills by developing local capacity.

Getting them to understand—getting the exchange participants to understand the United States better is really secondary or even tertiary. It is about building local capacity, inoculating against adversarial information or experiences.

So you add to that various other efforts, even the broader public diplomacy realm or the various efforts in global affairs or even their elements of counterterrorism or the narcotics, INL [Bureau of International Narcotics and Law Enforcement Affairs], there are a tremendous number of activities there that are operating in a silo.

And I think they do not just further our foreign policy in the economic sense and societal sense but definitely contribute to developing partner capacity on the ground.

Ms. SPEIER. I am going to interrupt you for a moment because I have only got a minute 30, and I want you each to answer this question. I serve on the House Permanent Select Committee on Intelligence, as does Ms. Stefanik. What message would you want to convey to the members of that committee in terms of the Russian influence and its potential impacts in this country?

Mr. ARMSTRONG. That it is severe, we are underestimating it, and there is no cost to the Russians for them doing it.

Mr. LUMPKIN. And mine would be to reinvest the IC in their capabilities to monitor, detect, and understand what the Russians are doing.

Mr. THOMAS. And I would add that it is probably just unknown here just how insidious, if that is the right word, the effort is in other countries overseas. I know there was one country in the Baltics who said propaganda and information influence is like carbon monoxide. It is colorless, it is odorless, and it comes in and does its job.

And it is a very interesting way to think about how propaganda is being used over there, especially in those countries where when a TV, a cable package is put together and within that package is Russian TV so that those people are getting simply a different point of view that is in key areas too, it is along the borders there with Russia. So there is much to consider there.

Ms. SPEIER. Thank you.

Thank you, Madam Chair.

Ms. STEFANIK. Thank you to all of the members from both sides of the aisle for such thoughtful questions. As you can see, there is an increased interest in these important issues.

I want to also thank our witnesses, Mr. Armstrong, Mr. Lumpkin, and Mr. Thomas. We look forward to continuing working with you as we begin the process of this year's NDAA, and thank you very much for your testimony today.

The meeting is adjourned.

[Whereupon, at 5:54 p.m., the subcommittee was adjourned.]

APPENDIX

Mᴀʀᴄʜ 15, 2017

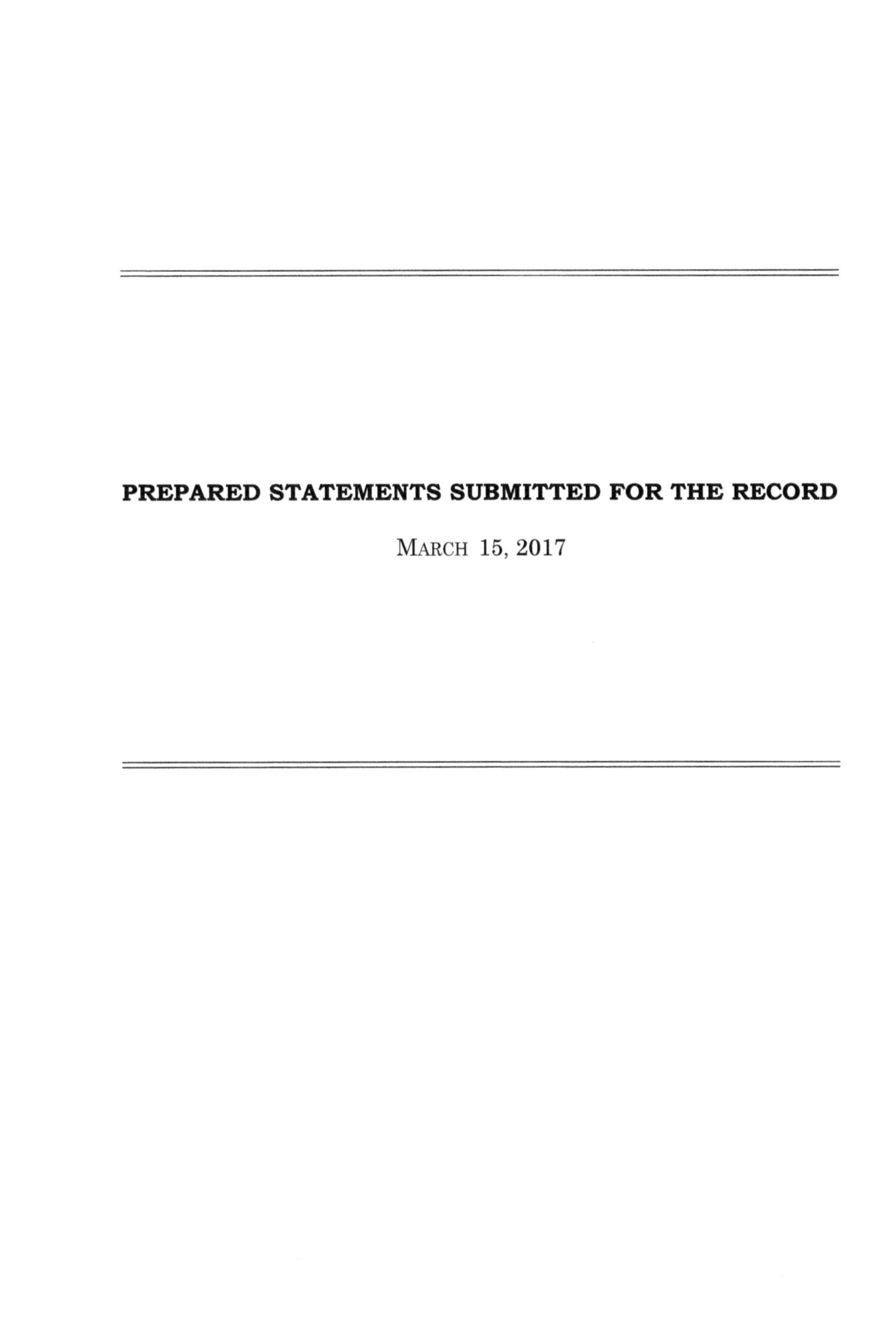

PREPARED STATEMENTS SUBMITTED FOR THE RECORD

MARCH 15, 2017

The subcommittee will come to order.

I'd like to welcome everyone to this hearing of the Emerging Threats and Capabilities Subcommittee of the House Armed Services Committee on the very timely topic of Information Warfare and Counter-Propaganda.

Although this subcommittee has met several times already in close-classified sessions, today is our first open and public hearing. As such, I'd like to take a moment to welcome and thank our new and returning subcommittee members, and also to congratulate our recently named Vice Chairwoman, Liz Cheney.

Our topic today is incredibly important: cyber warfare and influence campaigns that are being waged against our country represent a national security challenge of generational proportions.

In talking about influence campaigns, we too often focus on the digital and technical aspects; on the internet and social media. While those aspects are critical—and indeed have served as an accelerant to speed up communications and effects—we should remember to take a step back, and keep in mind that information warfare is about **information,** not just the medium; and our understanding of this form of warfare should also include the psychological, cognitive, and cultural aspects of the messages bombarding us from all sources.

I'd like to read a quote I recently reviewed:

> *"There has never been a time in our history when there was so great a need for our citizens to be informed and to understand what is happening in the world. The cause of freedom is being challenged throughout the world today...and propaganda is one of the most powerful weapons [they] have in this struggle. Deceit, distortion, and lies are systematically used by them as a matter of deliberate policy."*

Those were the words of President Harry Truman in 1950. He spoke of a conflict of ideas that is still occurring today. And unfortunately—it is a conflict we have largely ignored. I chose this quote as a reminder that Information Warfare and propaganda efforts are not new. The tools have changed, but enemy doctrine has not. Information warfare is shaping the international environment. There may not be overt and open fighting, but there is certainly open **conflict.** Information warfare is being waged in an aggressive ongoing competition over territory, resources, and people; in the Crimea; in the South China Sea; in Iraq, and in Syria.

People are being desensitized to the reality of actions around them, increasing the likelihood of misunderstanding and miscalculation.

Our core values of truth, democratic principles, and self-determination are under assault.

While the Department of Defense plays a critical role in this form of warfare, it cannot bear responsibility alone. Countering adversarial propaganda requires a whole-of-government strategy using all instruments of national power, to harness the authorities, tools and resources required to mitigate and marginalize its harmful effects.

With this in mind, the National Defense Authorization Act last year authorized and expanded the mission of the State Department's Global Engagement Center to counter **state-sponsored** propaganda efforts, such as Russia, China, Iran, and North Korea. We look forward to continuing to work with the Center and the Department of Defense this year, as we craft an Information Warfare and Counter-Propaganda strategy for an emerging security environment.

Before I turn to the Ranking Member for his comments, I'd like to highlight a few questions for our witnesses and Members to consider as we proceed throughout the hearing:

First, do we have an adequate strategy for countering the blatant lies and mistruths being promulgated by sophisticated nation-state actors that have both resources and political will?

Second, do we truly understand the Information Warfare and propaganda strategies of our enemies, be they state or non-state actors?

And lastly, since the United States remains a technological leader and innovator with tremendous creativity, how do we better harness our advantages to counter our adversaries?

Let me now turn to Ranking Member Jim Langevin of Rhode Island for any opening comments he'd like to make.

House Armed Services Committee Written Testimony
Hearing on Crafting an Information Warfare and Counter-Propaganda Strategy
for the Emerging Security Environment
March 15, 2017

Written Testimony By
Matthew Armstrong

The Past, Present, and Future of the War for Public Opinion
By Matthew Armstrong
January 19, 2017
Source: https://warontherocks.com/2017/01/the-past-present-and-future-of-the-war-for-public-opinion/

As resolutions do, Senate Resolution 74 opened with a declaration of fact:

> Whereas the first weapon of aggression by the Kremlin is propaganda designed to subvert, to confuse and to divide the free world, and to inflame the Russian and satellite peoples with hatred for our free institutions…

While these words sound familiar, this resolution is not of recent vintage. It was passed in June 1951 and launched several Congressional investigations into America's failing response to an expanding nonmilitary war.

Our world today is remarkably similar to that of the "cold war," before the era became a capitalized proper noun describing a bipolar order on the brink of nuclear disaster. Today, Russia, China, and the so-called Islamic State lead prominent efforts to "subvert, to confuse and to divide" their opposition while the West, and the United States in particular, remains largely unarmed in this struggle for minds and wills.

Testifying before the Senate Armed Services Committee recently, Director of National Intelligence James Clapper recommended a U.S. Information Agency (USIA) "on steroids," in reference to the Cold War-era agency designed to centralize the U.S. government's international information programs. These calls should be seen as yet another indictment of an aloof State Department that is not up to the present challenge.

While suggestions for a new agency concerned with influence and information are commonly put forward, they reveal how little we know of what the USIA was and what it was not. It was not a kind of Captain America's shield against political warfare. The concerns raised in the 1951 Senate resolution persisted throughout the decade as the USIA, the State Department, and foreign aid activities failed to anticipate Soviet tactics for a variety of reasons, from a lack of training to bureaucratic lethargy. Even as the Cold War raged, the United States was never properly prepared for the cold reality of the political warfare it was embroiled in. Therefore, we have no real historical precedent to draw upon today.

Public Opinion Matters: The Origins of the USIA

You can call it "information warfare," "hybrid warfare," or "political warfare," but whatever you call it, an adversary's attempts to shape the minds and will of people toward a political end is not new to the United States. Nor will this be the first time the United States sought to wield these weapons against its foes. An April 1918 report by the U.S. Army General Staff recognized that in the "strategic equation" of war there are "four factors — combat, economic, political, and psychologic — and that the last of these is coequal with the others." This is the early version of what we now call the DIME model of national power — diplomacy, information, military, economic. A July 1945 report from the State Department recognized that the "nature of present day foreign relations makes it essential for the United States to maintain informational activities abroad as an integral part of the conduct of our foreign affairs." Two years later, a Joint Congressional report elucidated on the growing threat:

> Europe today has again become a vast battlefield of ideologies in which words have replaced armaments as the active elements of attack and defense. The USSR and its obedient Communist parties throughout Europe have taken the initiative in this war of words against the western democracies.

Peace between nations, it was believed, came from mutual understanding. As Gen. Dwight D. Eisenhower testified in 1947, "real security, in contrast to the relative security of armaments, could develop only from understanding and mutual comprehension." U.S. information programs did not operate in a vacuum, but rather they complemented policy. To counter propaganda against the West, the U.S. government needed to make known the true purpose and nature of its policies, its society, and its people. There was more to it than simply exchanging information and culture.

American foreign aid, including the European Recovery Program, or Marshall Plan, was directed against "hunger, poverty, desperation and chaos," as Secretary of State George Marshall announced in June 1947. It sought to permit "the emergence of political and social conditions in which free institutions can exist." In a classified memo a few weeks later, George Kennan went further, describing the goal of the program as providing:

> a sense of political security, and of confidence in a future marked by close association with the Western Powers, [that] would itself release extensive recuperative forces in Europe which are today inhibited or paralyzed by political uncertainty. In this sense, we must recognize that much of the value of a European recovery program will lie not so much in its direct economic effects, which are difficult to calculate with any degree of accuracy, as in its psychological political by-products.

Foreign aid could not stand on its own. It had to be complemented by information efforts to deny the Communists from owning the narrative of the source and purpose of the aid. A few months later, Rep. Karl E. Mundt put it this way:

> We may help avert starvation in Europe and aid in producing a generation of healthy, physically fit individuals whose bodies are strong but whose minds are poisoned against America and whose loyalties are attached to the red star of Russia. If we permit this to eventuate it will be clear that the generosity of America is excelled only by our own stupidity.

With the Smith-Mundt Act of 1948, Congress fully authorized a global public affairs program run out of the State Department. This would be short-lived as the public affairs bullhorn placed in the State Department's hands proved to be inadequate against the rising pace and tenor of Communist efforts. Moreover, the State Department was not enthusiastic about this mission. It preferred to focus on diplomacy, which – to Foggy Bottom – was not a public affair.

As he ran for president, Eisenhower declared his frustration with a State Department that was plodding along on its own course, out of touch with the requirements of international affairs. He was frustrated to find the Mutual Security Administration equally disengaged from the management of foreign aid, including the massive Marshall Plan:

> We shall no longer have a Department of State that deals with foreign policy in an aloof cloister; a defense establishment that makes military appraisal in a vacuum; a Mutual Security Administration that, with sovereign independence, spends billions overseas. We must bring the dozens of agencies and bureaus into concerted action under an overall scheme of strategy. And we must have a firm hand on the tiller to sail the ship along a consistent course.

Once in office, in 1953 President Eisenhower implemented a whole of government approach through Reorganization Plans No. 7 and No. 8. In effect, Ike reorganized government around the DIME model. Plan No. 7 consolidated foreign affairs and aid activities under one organization, a hybrid of an independent agency that brought together Treasury, Defense, and State, largely under State's direction. Plan No. 8 created the USIA, centralizing America's public affairs operations under one agency, one leader, and one Congressional appropriation. State supported the reorganizations to return to what it viewed as its "traditional" role in diplomacy.

This new agency had a global impact, but not for the reasons that most people today think. It was not its radio network, but rather its "ground troops" – public affairs officers – who made the real difference. The public affairs sections in each U.S. embassy and consulate reported to the head of the USIA – not to the ambassador as they do now. The agency produced movies, books, pamphlets, posters, hosted talks and exchanges (academics, scientists, technicians, entertainers, and even bureaucrats). It worked to not just develop an understanding of America and its policies, but to develop the "political security" and confidence in the future that Marshall spoke of. An extensive network of libraries supported this work, providing a place for foreign publics to gather, read magazines and books, watch films, discuss anything, and attend classes. The USIA also produced radio programing, but this was secondary to the "ground game." As Edward R. Murrow described the agency's challenge,

The real art in this business is not so much moving information or guidance or policy five or 10,000 miles. That is an electronic problem. The real art is to move it the last three feet in face to face conversation.

Amateurs vs. Professionals: The Struggle for Minds and Wills
While USIA products were used domestically in the early Cold War, the agency was not, however, focused on defending and protecting American public opinion and perception. To fill that gap, in the 1950's, after USIA was created, the United States came close to developing a research and training program to develop the necessary skills and focus on defending the nation against forms of non-military aggression. It started as a private effort and not from the world of clandestine and covert operations. A group of Floridians that named themselves the Orlando Committee, led by a World War II paratrooper and Harvard graduate who previously taught a course on the subversive tactics of a then-unknown Mao Tse-Tung, recognized a near complete absence in educating Americans on the political techniques of Communists, both at home and abroad. Congress picked up on the effort and, with broad bipartisan support including sponsors Senators Paul H. Douglas, Thomas J. Dodd, Mundt (now in the Senate), and Representatives Judd and Herlong, a bill was introduced to establish the "Freedom Academy." Students would fall into three general categories: U.S. government officials whose agencies were involved in the U.S. effort to resist communism abroad; leaders from civil society, ranging from management to labor to education to fraternal and professional groups; and, leaders and potential leaders in and out of government from foreign countries. The Freedom Academy was to be strictly a research and educational institution and would not engage in any operational activities.

Mundt explained the need for the academy:

> [W]e train and prepare our military people for the war which we are not fighting and which we hope will never come, but we fail to train our own citizens and our representatives abroad to operate in the cold war — the only war which we are presently fighting.

But the Freedom Academy never came to be, though a Gallup poll showed that a remarkable 70 percent of the public knew of the bill to create it and supported it. The State Department strongly objected to the initiative primarily because it viewed the Freedom Academy as infringing on its primacy in foreign affairs. However, the State Department did not kill the Freedom Academy. No, the death blow came from a senator.

J. William Fulbright, the chairman of the Senate Foreign Relations Committee, pulled the Freedom Academy bill out of the Judiciary Committee and into his committee to let it die. He then admonished his colleagues that we "must learn to overcome our emotional prejudices against Russia" so that in time the Communists will learn to trust us. "I refuse to admit that the Communist dogma *per se* is a threat to the United States."

Fulbright did not stop there. Never a fan of USIA, by 1967 he was actively opposing the agency, and by 1972 was waging an all-out war against it, including replacing its permanent authorization with a requirement of an annual reauthorization. That year, Sen. James L. Buckley, showed a USIA film about Czechoslovakia on his monthly television show in New York. The U.S. attorney general held this activity to be permissible under the Smith-Mundt Act. Fulbright reacted by amending the law to block Americans – including the press and the Congress – from accessing USIA material. In doing so, he reframed the legislation into the "anti-propaganda" law many have thought of it since, tainting public diplomacy and other international information efforts.

In a perverse twist, by blocking the development and deployment of civilian and overt activities, Fulbright's actions on the Freedom Academy and the Smith-Mundt Act have done more to militarize American foreign policy than any other single act by denying Congress, policymakers, and practitioners critical experience, methods, and historical precedent to properly defend the nation through nonmilitary means. Further, it denied what would have been a shove to the State Department to lean into foreign policy and to adopt a culture of professional training.

The End of the USIA
The Cold War ended and the USIA came to be seen by some as obsolete. In 1999, it was abolished and broken into pieces. The bulk of its operations returned to the State Department. The broadcast operations, however, were spun out into an independent agency, currently named the Broadcasting Board of Governors (BBG). The BBG is a news organization purposefully distant from political messaging. It only partially fulfills Murrow's "electronic problem" as it strictly engages countries that have a severely limited or absent free press and is prohibited from operating in countries where it would compete with Western news media. These are markets that require a physical presence to provide local reporting and have high operating costs with limited to no commercial potential. It is far from a bulwark against the political warfare of American adversaries, especially when they operate inside the territory of America's closest allies in Europe and Asia.

The majority of the former USIA – whether measured in terms of staff, budget, or nations reached – exist today in the State Department. These are the public affairs sections in the U.S. embassies and consulates abroad, the Bureau of International Information Programs (IIP), and the Bureau of Educational and Cultural Affairs (ECA). All of these are under-resourced, under-staffed, poorly tasked, and usually lacking appropriate leadership. The foreign service officers and civil servants working in these areas are poorly supported professionally, denied essential training, and often prevented from focusing on the "last three feet"— face-to-face conversation. They tend to be occupied with administration and management functions. The State Department's public affairs sections abroad are under the authority of the ambassador, in contrast to the former USIA's public affairs sections that were under the Director of the USIA. The USIA equivalent of IIP, arguably the second largest group of functions of the late agency, provided integrated media development in support of public affairs sections. It also supported an extensive library system, now severely restricted under the State Department's security requirements. The products included publishing books and magazines, producing movies, and printing maps and posters. The USIA also offered speaking tours abroad of U.S. professionals and cultural icons to meet with locals directly. These continue today, but as the IPP's primary role shifted to develop social media packages for embassies, including an "all-hands" effort to promote tourism, its legacy as the core of USIA is all but forgotten.

The ECA, which manages overseas exchanges of all kinds, seems to be on auto-pilot, seemingly focused on exchanges for the sake of exchanges. Its decades old "Interagency Working Group," created to better coordinate exchanges sponsored by a myriad of government agencies, does little but create more busy work for the already overworked public affairs sections. While many officials realize that exchanges are essential in developing mutual understanding, its role in developing local capacity and building networks against adversarial politics is too often forgotten.

Whether it is a lack of strategic focus or empire-building within the State Department, or both, some of the former USIA roles have been distributed to yet other offices in the State Department, or recreated.

However, if you look closely today, you may see that Congress did "recreate" the USIA. They just call it the Global Engagement Center (GEC) and they placed it in the State Department. The GEC was previously established under an Executive Order until Congress made it "permanent" through legislation. It is charged with developing, planning, and synchronizing, "in coordination with the Secretary of Defense, and the heads of other relevant Federal departments and agencies" programs to identify and counter foreign propaganda and disinformation directed at "United States national security interests." Like any effort, the GEC's success depends on the quality of its staff, most of whom are contractors and detailees from the Defense Department. There are few foreign service officers inside the GEC, being both too few in number to spare and generally untrained in the necessary skills.

It is easy to charge the department with being "aloof" yet again: when was the last time a Secretary of State or Under Secretary went to Capitol Hill and asked for more public diplomacy staff? Or, more training and resources for public diplomacy?

While the USIA excelled at that "last three feet," it did not have the personnel, the funding, support, training, or mandate to match the vast Communist efforts to undermine democratic societies. It is unrealistic to imagine that creating a new organization will magically manifest the necessary staffing levels with the required skills, tactics, techniques, and procedures necessary to pre-empt and counter today's political warfare. Indeed, history shows that when we did create a new organization – USIA – that the development of the necessary capabilities and leadership to be effective in the struggle of minds and wills was not included.

Preparing for the War We Want or the War We Are In

If confirmed, Rex Tillerson, President-Elect Trump's nominee for secretary of state, will have a challenge ahead of him to get our State Department to reorganize and accept the role of information in international affairs. History is not on his side.

The new secretary of state will need to deal with not only the marginal role the State Department allows for "public diplomacy," but also the lack of professional training of the Foreign Service on the role of public opinion in international affairs. Where professional education is required in the military for advancement, with the exception of language or cultural training for the next assignment, it is a derogatory interruption of a career path in the Foreign Service. More specifically, issues related to political warfare are not framed in terms of foreign policy but national security, placing them squarely in the domain of the military. It is the military that supports the detailed analysis and discussion of these issues as they look to learn from the past and present to prepare for the future in a professional education system that includes many schools (which the Foreign Service does attend) and many more journals. It should also be noted that the Congressional Armed Services Committees spend significant time on subject of political warfare and it is here that the GEC legislation originated (as well as the rollback of Fulbright's perversion of the Smith-Mundt Act). If we are to de-militarize our foreign policy, we must look to raise the capacity of the nonmilitary foreign affairs community to delve into these topics. Inquiry by the appropriate oversight committees in Congress must also increase to better understand the requirements to train and fund efforts to pre-empt, mitigate, and negate the political warfare waged against us. We cannot afford to continue to rely on the Defense Department to compensate for an "aloof" State Department

I recently attended a conference at King's College London on the informational aspect of "hybrid warfare" that was attended by Russian professors teaching the current and future foreign service of Russia. The Russians were interested in what they described as our militaristic view of foreign policy. They cited as examples the writings of Frank Hoffman on hybrid warfare that are published in military-centric journals with military-centric themes for military-related audiences. There are strikingly few non-military options that support and publish national security writing for thoughtful thinkers like Hoffman. More to the point, there is virtually no professional education for our foreign service to grant the time and money to dig into these topics, nor are they prepared before entry into the foreign service by the schools that focus on preparing them for the foreign service. These realities contribute to a further militarization of our approach to national security. The Russians, meanwhile, appear to working on their own "Freedom Academy."

The stakes today are higher as the cost of failure has increased as public opinion, influenced by both increased transparency and disinformation, has an increasing influence on domestic and foreign policy. Societal, economic, and political disruption no longer requires the resources of a national government, while phrases like "self-radicalization" masks the effectiveness of foreign (ideological, geographical, cultural, or political) agents. "If a country is lost to communism," George Gallup wrote in 1962, "through propaganda and subversion it is lost to our side as irretrievably as if we had lost it in actual warfare." Through political warfare, the enemy not only gets a vote in the success of our policies, but they can rig the public opinion against us. We covered this ground before and the solution was not creating a new agency.

We should ask ourselves if we want to fix our State Department, or bypass it? Policies rely on information programs to not just be known, but to be effective, especially in the contemporary high-speed and transparent world. We disregard fundamental truths described by the Army nearly one hundred years ago, the State Department in 1945, and repeatedly by Members of Congress at our peril.

In their 1963 surrender letter following Fulbright's "success" in killing the Freedom Academy bill, the Orlando Committee held out hope. "Someday this nation will recognize that global non-military conflict must be pursued with the same intensity and preparation as global military conflicts." That day has yet to come.

Reprinted with permission from War on the Rocks:
https://warontherocks.com/2017/01/the-past-present-and-future-of-the-war-for-public-
opinion/

Matthew Armstrong

Mr. Matthew Armstrong is an author and advisor on public diplomacy, international information, and propaganda. His emphasis is examining how operating structures, authorities, doctrine, and individual opinions impact informational activities in support of national or organizational strategy with a focus on traditional and emerging security issues facing civilian and military government agencies. He is an Associate Fellow at King's Centre for Strategic Communication at King's College London.

From August 2013 through December 2016, he served as a Governor on the Broadcasting Board of Governors. He was nominated by the President and confirmed by the Senate into this part-time role where he provided strategic guidance and oversight over the Voice of America, Radio Free Europe / Radio Liberty, Radio Free Asia, Office of Cuba Broadcasting, and the Middle East Broadcasting Network. Collectively, and separate from the expansive Internet Freedom programs of the BBG and RFA, the networks operated in up to 61 languages in over 100 countries.

Since 2012, Mr. Armstrong has served as a Member of the Board of The Public Diplomacy Council, and since 2014 as the Board Secretary. The PDC is a nonprofit organization committed to the importance of the academic study, professional practice, and responsible advocacy of public diplomacy.

In 2011, Mr. Armstrong served as the Executive Director of the U.S. Advisory Commission on Public Diplomacy where he reoriented the organization to its core purpose of "advocacy and oversight over U.S. government efforts that intend to understand, inform, and influence foreign publics."

In 2010, he founded and led the MountainRunner Institute, a 501(c)3 non-profit focused on issues related to public diplomacy. In 2004, he launched the leading blog on public diplomacy and strategic communication, www.MountainRunner.us.

Mr. Armstrong is a member of the John Hays Initiative, DACOR, the Pen & Sword Club, and sits on several "small councils" advising various agencies and NATO-member ministries on issues related to strategic communication. He is on the editorial boards for the journal of the NATO Strategic Communications Centre of Excellence and the Journal of Strategic Security. He has been a member of the National Press Club since 2009.

He taught graduate courses on public diplomacy at the USC Annenberg School of Communication and Journalism, and continues to lecture and speak at U.S. military schools, NATO, and other military and civilian foreign government institutions across Europe and in Asia on strategic communication and public diplomacy. He has worked extensively with the Congress, think tanks, and the academic community across several continents on the same topics. In October 2015, he testified before a subcommittee of the U.S. House Armed Services Committee on the subject of emerging threats in today's information environment. In October 2016, he was made an Honorary Member of the PSYOP Regiment at Fort Bragg.

He is a Founding Board Member of the Lodestone Trust, a land conservation trust established in 2016 for the research and development of outdoor therapy for military service-related post-traumatic stress disorder patients under professional supervision; identifying, mentoring, and enabling outstanding entrepreneurs; and, preserving wilderness and wildlife habitat.

Prior to his work in foreign affairs, he developed and deployed enterprise knowledge management systems and was a director at a public relations and communications company.

Mr. Armstrong earned a B.A. in International Relations and a Master of Public Diplomacy from the University of Southern California. He also studied European security and the Middle East at the University of Wales, Aberystwyth.

He currently resides near Zürich, Switzerland, with his wife, two children, and dog (a rescue from a Romanian shelter).

DISCLOSURE FORM FOR WITNESSES
COMMITTEE ON ARMED SERVICES
U.S. HOUSE OF REPRESENTATIVES

INSTRUCTION TO WITNESSES: Rule 11, clause 2(g)(5), of the Rules of the U.S.
House of Representatives for the 115th Congress requires nongovernmental witnesses
appearing before House committees to include in their written statements a curriculum
vitae and a disclosure of the amount and source of any federal contracts or grants
(including subcontracts and subgrants), or contracts or payments originating with a
foreign government, received during the current and two previous calendar years either
by the witness or by an entity represented by the witness and related to the subject matter
of the hearing. This form is intended to assist witnesses appearing before the House
Committee on Armed Services in complying with the House rule. Please note that a copy
of these statements, with appropriate redactions to protect the witness's personal privacy
(including home address and phone number) will be made publicly available in electronic
form not later than one day after the witness's appearance before the committee.
Witnesses may list additional grants, contracts, or payments on additional sheets, if
necessary.

Witness name: _MATTHE Charles Armstrong_

Capacity in which appearing: (check one)

☑ Individual

☐ Representative

**If appearing in a representative capacity, name of the company, association or other
entity being represented:** ____

Federal Contract or Grant Information: If you or the entity you represent before the
Committee on Armed Services has contracts (including subcontracts) or grants (including
subgrants) with the federal government, please provide the following information:

2017

Federal grant/ contract	Federal agency	Dollar value	Subject of contract or grant
NONE			

2016

Federal grant/ contract	Federal agency	Dollar value	Subject of contract or grant
None			

2015

Federal grant/ contract	Federal agency	Dollar value	Subject of contract or grant
None			

Foreign Government Contract or Payment Information: If you or the entity you represent before the Committee on Armed Services has contracts or payments originating from a foreign government, please provide the following information:

2017

Foreign contract/ payment	Foreign government	Dollar value	Subject of contract or payment
€. 250	*NATO*	*$250*	*Editorial Board – NATO SC COE*

2016

Foreign contract/ payment	Foreign government	Dollar value	Subject of contract or payment
£ 750	NATO	$ 750	Editorial Board NATO SC COE

2015

Foreign contract/ payment	Foreign government	Dollar value	Subject of contract or payment

STATEMENT OF

HONORABLE MICHAEL D. LUMPKIN

PRINICIPAL

NEPTUNE

BEFORE THE 115TH CONGRESS

HOUSE ARMED SERVICES COMMITTEE

SUBCOMITTEE ON EMERGING THREATS AND CAPABILITIES

Introduction

Chairwoman Stefanik, Ranking Member Langevin, and distinguished members of the Committee, thank you for this opportunity to address you today as private citizen and in an individual capacity on the topic of *Crafting an Information Warfare and Counter-Propaganda Strategy for the Emerging Security Environment*. I trust my experience as a career special operations officer, Assistant Secretary of Defense for Special Operations and Low Intensity Conflict, and Special Envoy and Coordinator for the Global Engagement Center at the Department of State will be helpful in providing perspective on the current status of the U.S. government's strategy, capabilities, and direction in information warfare and counter-propaganda. The previous Administration and the 114th Congress demonstrated a clear commitment to this issue, as evidenced by the President Obama's Executive Order 13721 which established the Global Engagement Center (GEC) and the 2017 National Defense Authorization Act (NDAA) that expanded the Center's mission. The 2017 NDAA expanded the GEC's mandate to include counter-state propaganda and disinformation efforts, well beyond its original charter which limited it to diminishing the influence of terrorist organizations such as the Islamic State of Iraq and Syria (ISIS) in the information domain. This is a big step in the right direction, but the sobering fact is that we are still far from where we ultimately need to be to successfully operate in the modern information environment.

That said, I am very pleased to be joined here today by former governor of the Broadcast Board of Governors Matt Armstrong and Mr. Timothy Thomas from the U.S. Army Office of Foreign

Military Studies. I cannot think of any two people more knowledgeable in this area than the two individuals seated next to me. I believe we are collectively postured to address your questions on the issue at hand.

The Current Situation

Since the end of the Cold War with the Soviet Union which arguably was the last period in history when the US successfully engaged in sustained information warfare and counter-state propaganda efforts, technology and how the world communicates has changed dramatically. We now live in a hyper-connected world where the flow of information moves in real time. The lines of authority and effort between Public Diplomacy, Public Affairs, and Information Warfare have blurred to the point where in many cases information is consumed by US and foreign audiences at the same time via the same methods. To illustrate this fact, as this Committee is aware, it was 33-year-old IT consultant in Abbottabad, Pakistan that first reported the US military raid against Osama bin Laden in May of 2011 on Twitter. This happened as events were still unfolding on the ground and hours before the American people were officially notified by the President of the United States' address.

While the means and methods of communication have transformed significantly over the past decade, much of the US government thinking on shaping and responding in the information environment has remained unchanged, to include how we manage US government information dissemination and how we respond to the information of our adversaries. We are cognitively hamstrung for a myriad of reasons to include: lack of accountability and oversight, bureaucracy resulting in insufficient levels of resourcing and inability to absorb cutting-edge information and analytic tools, and access to highly skilled personnel.

Lack of Accountability and Oversight

To date, there is not a single individual in the US government below the President of the United States who is responsible and capable of managing US information dissemination and how we address our adversaries in the information environment. The 2017 NDAA mandated that GEC lead, organize, and synchronize U.S. government counter-propaganda and disinformation efforts against State and non-State actors abroad, but it fell short in elevating it to a position where it could fully execute its mission. The GEC operates at the Assistant Secretary level and lacks the authority to direct the Interagency. In practice, this means that the GEC is considered at best a peer to a half dozen regional or functional bureaus at the State Department and several disparate organizations at the Department of Defense, to say nothing of the other departments and agencies that have a stake in this fight. Furthermore, although the GEC is directed by law with the mission to lead the Interagency, its role is reduced to simply a "suggesting" function. It is then up to the respective agency whether to comply. This misalignment of responsibility, authority, and accountability will without doubt continue to hamper the efforts of the GEC until it is ultimately corrected by statute.

Before his departure as the Director of National Intelligence, Jim Clapper told this Congress that the United States needs to resurrect the old US Information Agency (USIA) and put it on steroids. While I agree with DNI Clapper that we need to increase our focus and management of the information environment, I do not believe that resurrecting the USIA in its previous form will allow the US government to be relevant in the ever-changing information landscape. While the USIA had many positives, there were also many challenges which ultimately resulted in its disestablishment. That said, DNI Clapper was figuratively closer to a solution than even he may have thought. Elevating the GEC and its role of leading, coordinating, and synchronizing US government efforts to something similar to what the Office of the Director of National Intelligence does with intelligence would bring alignment between responsibility, authority, and accountability while minimizing significant bureaucratic tension and cost.

Such an elevation in stature would allow the GEC to advocate for resourcing levels for the Interagency as well as drive a single information strategy and bring discipline to the US government efforts. Many talented people in government are working this issue thoughtfully and diligently, unfortunately they are not always working in unison because they are answering to different leaders with different priorities.

The Limitations of the Truth and Bureaucracy

It is not unreasonable to think that the United States will always be at some disadvantage against our adversaries in the information environment. We are a nation of laws where truth and ethics are expected, and rightly so. Our enemies on the contrary are not constrained by

ethics, the truth, or the law. Our adversaries, both State and non-State actors, can and will

bombard all forms of communications to include traditional media and social media with their

messages to influence, create doubt of our actions or intentions, and even recruit people to

their cause. We must ensure that we organize our efforts in such a manner that maximize

desired outcomes through discipline, agility, and innovation.

When using the terms agility and innovation, the US government is generally not the first thing

to comes to mind. This also holds true in the information environment. For example, it

remains difficult to introduce new social media analytic and forensic tools onto government IT

systems because of lengthy and highly complicated compliance processes. These tools are

critical to understanding the social media landscape and are required to ensure the US efforts

are hitting the right audience with the right message at the right time that influences thought

or behavior. Analytic tools are advancing as fast at the information environment itself and time

lateness for implementation can have a devastating effect.

These tools cost money and it takes significant resources to train on these ever-advancing

capabilities. While budgets for US government information warfare and counter-propaganda

efforts have increased significantly, they still pale to the resources applied to kinetic efforts. A

single kinetic strike against a single high value terrorist can tally into the hundreds of millions of

dollars when conducted outside an area of active armed hostilities (when adding intelligence

preparation before and after the strike) and in many cases, only have short term affects. At the same time the GEC funding in FY17 is below $40M.   Again, please keep in mind that this is a

significant increase from the GEC FY15 budget of $5.6M. We are making progress just not fast

enough to turn the tide in our favor any time soon as many of our adversaries are putting

significantly more resources into information operations than we are.

Even when fully resourced and masterfully executed, information warfare and counter-

propaganda efforts can contain a high element of risk. While bureaucracy in government is

necessary to standardize routine tasks, it cannot be left to control the totality of our efforts in

the information environment. The bureaucratic standard operating procedure strives to reduce

risk to almost zero which can ultimately lead to diluted messaging efforts that can result in

missing the right audience with an effective message that shifts their thought and behavior to

our desired end state. To be successful we must learn to accept a higher level of risk and

accept the fact that sometimes we are just going to get it wrong despite our best efforts. When

we do get it wrong, we must learn, adapt, and iterate our messaging rapidly to be relevant and

effective.

Access to Trained Personnel

As mentioned previously, there are some talented people in government working the

information environment challenge. There are, however, just not enough of them nor are they

always able to keep up with the technological advances in this arena. Some success has been

realized in using the Section 3161 hiring authority granted to the GEC by Executive Order

13721. This authority allows the GEC to hire limited term/limited scope employees directly into government based on their skills and capabilities. This has provided the GEC access to experienced private sector talent that government service does not traditionally provide. Access to the talent of academia, Silicon Valley, and Madison Avenue now is possible for the GEC. Unfortunately, outside of the GEC, other federal departments and agencies do not have the ability to leverage the Section 3161 hiring authority to access top talent in the field. The recent federal hiring "freeze" will exacerbate this challenge as new highly talented people are prevented from joining the federal workforce.

In Conclusion

Recognition of the importance of US government's role in the information environment continues to grow as exemplified by the creation and expansion of the GEC. Indeed, significant progress has made. It is imperative, however, that the government's efforts be fully coordinated and resourced to be responsive and adaptive. The information environment and our adversaries' actions will continue to evolve and our means and methods need to remain agile and innovative to stay relevant and effective in the emerging security environment.

Mr. Michael Lumpkin

Michael joined the Neptune Team after serving as Special Envoy/Coordinator at the U.S. State Department's Global Engagement Center, Assistant Secretary of Defense for Special Operations and Low Intensity Conflict, and Deputy Chief of Staff at the Department of Veteran's Affairs (VA).

During his time as a government civilian, Michael was trusted with the most challenging issues: spearheading the implementation of the 2010 Omnibus Caregivers Act, reorganizing the Department of Defense (DoD) POW/MIA recovery operations, leading the repatriation of Sgt. Bowe Bergdahl, overseeing the DoD Task Force that successfully responded to the Ebola outbreak in West Africa, and establishing the Global Engagement Center to counter violent extremists' online presence, propaganda and disinformation.

Prior to his administration appointments, Michael had a varied background serving as CEO at Industrial Security Alliance Partners, Director of Business Development at ATI, and served as a career naval officer. He is a qualified Surface Warfare Officer and Navy SEAL, serving in every leadership position within the teams from Platoon Commander to Team commanding officer, and is a veteran of Operation Iraqi Freedom and Operation Enduring Freedom.

A native of San Diego, he has well-established roots in Alexandria, Virginia and is living life to the fullest. A true frogman, he is an avid outdoorsman, and critter rescuer.

DISCLOSURE FORM FOR WITNESSES
COMMITTEE ON ARMED SERVICES
U.S. HOUSE OF REPRESENTATIVES

INSTRUCTION TO WITNESSES: Rule 11, clause 2(g)(5), of the Rules of the U.S. House of Representatives for the 115th Congress requires nongovernmental witnesses appearing before House committees to include in their written statements a curriculum vitae and a disclosure of the amount and source of any federal contracts or grants (including subcontracts and subgrants), or contracts or payments originating with a foreign government, received during the current and two previous calendar years either by the witness or by an entity represented by the witness and related to the subject matter of the hearing. This form is intended to assist witnesses appearing before the House Committee on Armed Services in complying with the House rule. Please note that a copy of these statements, with appropriate redactions to protect the witness's personal privacy (including home address and phone number) will be made publicly available in electronic form not later than one day after the witness's appearance before the committee. Witnesses may list additional grants, contracts, or payments on additional sheets, if necessary.

Witness name: Michael David Lumpkin

Capacity in which appearing: (check one)

☒ Individual

☐ Representative

If appearing in a representative capacity, name of the company, association or other entity being represented: ____

Federal Contract or Grant Information: If you or the entity you represent before the Committee on Armed Services has contracts (including subcontracts) or grants (including subgrants) with the federal government, please provide the following information:

2017

Federal grant/ contract	Federal agency	Dollar value	Subject of contract or grant
N/A			

2016

Federal grant/ contract	Federal agency	Dollar value	Subject of contract or grant
N/A			

2015

Federal grant/ contract	Federal agency	Dollar value	Subject of contract or grant
N/A			

<u>Foreign Government Contract or Payment Information</u>: If you or the entity you represent before the Committee on Armed Services has contracts or payments originating from a foreign government, please provide the following information:

2017

Foreign contract/ payment	Foreign government	Dollar value	Subject of contract or payment
N/A			

2016

Foreign contract/ payment	Foreign government	Dollar value	Subject of contract or payment
N/A			

2015

Foreign contract/ payment	Foreign government	Dollar value	Subject of contract or payment
N/A			

RECORD VERSION

STATEMENT BY

MR. TIMOTHY L. THOMAS
SENIOR ANALYST, FOREIGN MILITARY STUDIES OFFICE
FORT LEAVENWORTH, KS

BEFORE THE

HOUSE ARMED SERVICES COMMITTEE
SUBCOMMITTEE ON EMERGING THREATS and CAPABILITIES

FIRST SESSION, 115TH CONGRESS

ON RUSSIA'S INFORMATION WAR CONCEPTS

MARCH 15, 2017

NOT FOR PUBLICATION UNTIL RELEASED BY THE

COMMITTEE ON ARMED SERVICES

STATEMENT BY MR. TIMOTHY L. THOMAS

SENIOR ANALYST, FOREIGN MILITARY STUDIES OFFICE
FORT LEAVENWORTH, KS

RUSSIA'S VIEWS ON MODERN WARFARE AND USE OF INFORMATION OPERATIONS: THE INTEGRATION OF ROLES

Views on Modern Warfare

During the past three or four years Western analysts have tried to decipher Russian military actions and find a term to describe them. Two concepts in particular have dominated these discussions. The first is the issue of hybrid operations. Western analysts have not only labeled Russian actions as hybrid but also state that this is the wording Russia's military uses to describe their operations.[1] However, Russia states that it is the West who is using hybrid operations against Russia. Second, after 2013 the West added another descriptor to their assessment of Russian military actions, labeling Russia's operations to be examples of new-generation wars (NGW). As opposed to the hybrid label, for which there was no hard evidence, the NGW label is based on wording used by Russian military authors to describe future methods of conducting warfare. In 2013 Russian military officers on several occasions referred to NGW, with two authors in particular using the term as the title of their joint article. However, ever since 2013, the Russian military has gone silent on the topic of NGW and for the past two years the Russian military has been using the term new-type wars (NTW).

Hybrid Thought

In 2014 and 2015 many Westerners increasingly referred to Russian actions in Ukraine as part of a hybrid war that included the use of hard and soft tactics to achieve the goals of Russian President Vladimir Putin and the military. However, Russia's military makes the opposite assertion, that the West is using hybrid tactics against Russia. For example, with regard to hybrid war, a *Military Thought* article in 2015 by two Russian authors stated the following:

> 'Hybrid warfare (gibridnaya voyna),' then, is not exactly the right term and is slightly at odds with the glossary used in this country's military science. Essentially, these actions can be regarded as a form of confrontation between countries or, in a narrow sense, as a form in which forces and capabilities are used to assure national security.[2]

---

[1] See, for example, Dovydas Pancerovas, "Russia's Sixth Column in Lithuania is a Sign Russia is Already Conducting Hybrid War in Our Country, Too," *15min.lt*, 23 September 2014.

[2] V. B. Andrianov and V. V. Loyko, "Questions Regarding the Use of the Armed Forces of the Russian Federation in Crisis Situations in Peacetime," *Voennaya Mysl' (Military Thought)*, No. 1 2015, p. 68.

If you template your own thought process, such as hybrid thought, onto another nations, you might totally miss their key assessment and decision-making criteria, follow a wrong path, or make unforced errors. Thinking your opponent is using your thought process is mirror-imaging.

New-Generation War

In 2013 several articles appeared that mentioned the NGW concept. A full explanation of the concept was first provided in a 2013 article titled, "The Nature and Content of a New-Generation War." The authors, S. A. Chekinov and S. G. Bogdanov, who had earlier discussed indirect and asymmetric operations in detail, described the "way" in which a future war might be fought.[3] Initially Chekinov and Bogdanov described NGW as based on nonmilitary options, mobile joint forces, and new information technologies. They offered seven points for consideration.

First, the aggressive side would use nonmilitary actions as it plans to attack its victim in a NGW.[4] **Second**, decisive battles will rage in the information environment, where the attacker manipulates the "intelligent machines" at a distance. A quantum computer may turn into a tool of destruction in this sense, as new-generation "blitz" wars will be created, operating in the nanosecond range. **Third**, the aggressor may use nonlethal, new-generation, genetically engineered biological weapons that affect the human psyche and moods, which intensify propaganda effects and thereby help to drag the target country into chaos and disobedience among the population.[5] (Russian authors appear to fear this happening inside their country. They write often on the fear of so-called "color revolutions" occurring.)

Fourth, the start of the military phase will be preceded by large-scale reconnaissance and subversive missions conducted under the guise of information operations. These operations will be used to target important objectives vital to the country's sustainability.[6] **Fifth**, the attack will probably begin with an aerospace operation lasting several days. The goal will be to damage an opponent's key military and industrial capabilities, communication hubs, and military control centers.[7] **Sixth**, the defender must anticipate an attack by military robots in conjunction with the aerospace attack. This implies the extended use of UAVs first of all, as well as robot-controlled systems capable of engaging in combat activities independently.[8] **Seventh,** the authors relate that the opening period of a NGW will be pivotal, breaking it down into several phases, to include targeted information operations, electronic warfare operations, aerospace operations, and the use of precision weaponry, long-range artillery, and weapons based on new physical

---

[3] S. G. Chekinov and S. A. Bogdanov, "The Nature and Content of a New–Generation War," *Voennaya Mysl'* (*Military Thought*), No. 10 2013, pp. 13-25.
[4] Ibid., p. 19.
[5] Ibid., 21.
[6] Ibid.
[7] Ibid.
[8] Ibid., 22.

principles. In the closing period of war attackers will roll over any remaining points of resistance and destroy surviving enemy units with special operations.[9]

The authors concluded by stating that "a country preaching a defensive doctrine may get the short end of the deal in the face of a surprise attack by an aggressor."[10] Information superiority and anticipatory operations will be the main ingredients for success in NGWs.[11] For the past 1500 days, however, the term NGW has not appeared in Russia's military press to the best of my knowledge.

New-Type Warfare

In early 2015, in the *Bulletin of the Academy of Military Science* of Russia, General-Lieutenant A. V. Kartapalov, then the Chief of the Main Operations Directorate of the General Staff of Russia (in late 2015 he was named as the head of the Western Military District), wrote a lengthy article on the recent lessons of military conflicts and what they had taught Russia. The article examines changes in the nature of armed struggle and what is described as "new warfare" or "war of a new type."[12]

Kartapolov noted that increasingly the U.S. is using hybrid operations, which include military and non-military measures. These measures are accompanied by dynamic information-psychological effects against the population and leadership of victim states; by the use of armed internal opposition detachments; and by the use of special operations forces [author: which mimic almost perfectly Russian actions in Ukraine]. Russia calls such actions "indirect." They differ from "direct" operations, since the latter must be especially dynamic and not passive in any form according to Kartapalov.[13]

The potential capabilities of the U.S. military were especially underscored by Kartapalov. He stated that America's basing systems abroad, its global missile defense architecture and instantaneous global strike concept (which presupposes strategic and non-nuclear precision weapons), and its precision electronic information strikes and technical development of a reconnaissance-strike system have all been created or improved. These actions in Kartapalov's opinion can undermine global stability, disrupt the correlation of forces in the nuclear missile sphere, and create a real threat in the mid-term to the security of the Russian Federation.[14]

To balance the technological superiority of countries, such as the U.S., nonstandard forms and methods are being developed. Russia's new-type warfare includes "asymmetric" methods for confronting an enemy. Measures include the use of Special Forces operations, foreign agents, various forms of information effects, and other

---

[9] Ibid., 23.

[10] Ibid., p. 23.

[11] Ibid.

[12] A. V. Kartapalov, "Lessons of Military Conflicts and Prospects for the Development of Means and Methods of Conducting Them, Direct and Indirect Actions in Contemporary International Conflicts," *Vestnik Akademii Voennykh Nauk (Bulletin of the Academy of Military Science)*, No. 2 2015, pp. 26-36.

[13] Ibid., p. 29.

[14] Ibid., p. 35.

nonmilitary forms of effects. For each conflict a different set of asymmetric operations will be created. Such actions must be timely and coordinated with respect to targets, location, and time in regard to various departments of government organizations.[15] Kartapalov notes that asymmetric operations "are inherent to a conflict situation in which by means of actions of an economic, diplomatic, informational, and indirect military nature a weaker enemy uses an asymmetric strategy (tactics) to conduct an armed struggle in accordance with his available limited resources to level the stronger side's military-technological superiority."[16]

As a result, indirect and asymmetric actions must be included in the appropriate regulations and provisions, and they must be introduced into the operational training of forces in military schools and institutes.[17] Kartapalov noted that asymmetric actions are conducted with the aim of eliminating (neutralizing) advantages the enemy has and delivering against him (subjecting him to) damage using minimal expenditures, to include: covertness of preparation for the conduct of operations; persuasion of the weak side to use prohibited means to conduct military operations; concentration of efforts against the enemy's most vulnerable locations (targets); searching for and expose the enemy's weak points; imposing on the enemy one's own variant (one's own will) for the course of the conflict; and expending low resources with respect to enemy actions. The goal is to achieve superiority or parity with results.[18] The diagram below is the only template Russia's military has offered on distinct phases of a modern war, termed a new-type war, to which Russia subscribes, according to Kartapolov:

---

[15] Ibid., p. 36.
[16] Ibid., p. 35.
[17] Ibid., p. 36.
[18] Ibid., p. 35.

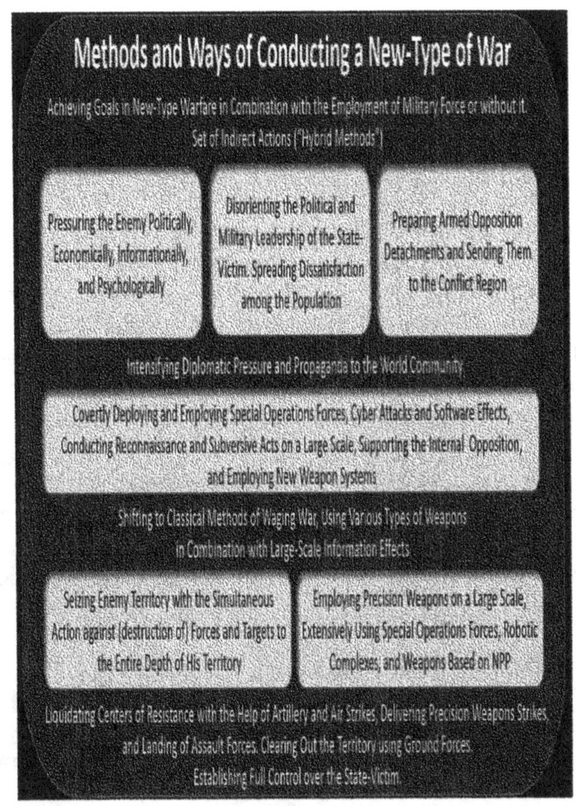

Russia's Indirect/Asymmetric Plans

General of the Army Makhmut Gareev, the President of the Academy of Military Science, introduced the concept of strategic deterrence. He defined this asymmetric approach as part of a set of interrelated political, diplomatic, information, economic, military, and other measures that deter, reduce, or avert threats and aggressive actions by any state or coalition of states with threats of unacceptable consequences as a result of retaliatory actions.[19] He offered the asymmetrical method of destroying an opponent's unified information space, sources of intelligence, navigation and guidance systems, and communications and command and control systems instead of fighting with ground forces."[20]

---

[19] M. A. Gareev, "Strategic Deterrence: Problems and Solutions," *Krasnaya Zvezda (Red Star),* No. 183, 8 October 2008, p. 8, as downloaded from Eastview.com on 17 March, 2010.
[20] Ibid.

With regard to indirect actions, Gareev stated one must understand "the correlation of direct and indirect actions in strategy. Indirect actions are tied to political, economic, and psychological influences on the enemy and to methods of feeding him disinformation and destroying him from within...We are talking about a greater flexibility in military art...including nonmilitary and nontraditional ones."[21]

S. G. Chekinov and S. A. Bogdanov, the NGW authors, stated that the re-division of territory and markets is now being achieved through the indirect approach and the employment of nonmilitary means. The indirect approach strategy uses various forms and methods of indirect military and nonmilitary actions and means, to include information, noncontact confrontation, electronic, fire-based, land-sea, and aerospace attacks. Nonmilitary means include political, legal, economic standards, spiritual values, general-purpose information, and technological systems used by the state to influence internal and external relations. States that cannot secure their information security risk losing their political sovereignty, economic independence, and cannot aspire to be even regional leaders. This may require studying more closely the foreign experience in information operations.[22] Asymmetrical approaches feature a combination of forms and methods of using forces and means to exploit areas where adversaries have an unequal combat potential as compared to Russia. The use of such means allows for the avoidance of a direct confrontation.[23]

Deterrence: An Indirect/Asymmetric Vector?

It appears that Russia is utilizing a series of deterrent concepts intended to prevent the use of armed force against Russia, and to protect its sovereignty and territorial integrity.[24] Russia has two terms for deterrence, *sderzhivanie* and *ustrashenie.* The military uses the former much more often than the latter. *Sderzhivanie* is defined as the deterrence of containment. It is used to limit the development of weapons or the use of military actions. U*strashit'* is defined as deterrence through intimidation. It is used to frighten someone via fear. In effect, the terms seem to be complimentary. Frightening someone can result in their containment. Containing someone can result in their being frightened. Two examples are provided here, namely information and space deterrence:

Information: In November 2015, Russian TV carried images of supposed "top secret" schematics of a Russian naval torpedo, the Status-6. The torpedo allegedly carries nuclear warheads and supposedly can travel up to 10,000 kilometers, making it capable of striking the western shores of the US and creating a tsunami in the process. The Russian press labeled this action as "deliberate stove piping," that is, an attempt to scare analysts with a deliberate release of information. The torpedo would be impossible for

---

[21] M.A. Gareev: "Lessons and Conclusions Drawn From the Experience of the Great Patriotic War for Building Up and Training the Armed Forces," *Voennaya Mysl' (Military Thought)*, No. 5 2010, p. 20.

[22] S. G. Chekinov and S. A. Bogdanov, "The Strategy of the Indirect Approach: Its Impact on Modern Warfare," *Voennaya Mysl' (Military Thought)*, No. 6 2011, pp. 3-13.

[23] Ibid.

[24] *On the Russian Federation's National Security Strategy, President of Russia's Website*, 31 December 2015.

either Prompt Global Strike or a Global ABM to detect or intercept. Of interest is that the torpedo's development may not even be complete, [25] but just the suggestion of such a capability can help to deter an opponent, who is uncertain as to the validity of the claim. A month later Russia stated that it's "Rus" deep-diving submersible, part of the secret Defense Ministry's Main Directorate for Deep-Sea Research, had transmitted information from NATO's underwater intercontinental communications cables. The Rus can descend to 6,000 meters with a crew of three hydronauts, where it can carry out technical, emergency rescue, photography, video filming, or scientific research operations.[26]

Space Maneuvering: A Russian satellite "parked itself between two Intelsat satellites in geosynchronous orbit for five months this year" and maneuvered at times to within ten kilometers of these vehicles.[27] Roscosmos declined to comment on the matter, and the Russian Defense Ministry said it would "look into the situation."[28] This maneuvering was designed to imply capabilities to offset the Prompt Global Strike and Global ABM concepts that are seen as direct threats to Russia. In addition, Strategic Missile Force commander Karakayev noted that plans envisage fundamentally new means and techniques for penetrating any missile defense system.[29]

Information Operations

As Defense Minister Shoygu stated, words, cameras, photos, the Internet, and other types of information can become weapons on their own. These weapons can serve, in the hands of an investigator, prosecutor, or judge, he notes, as elements that change the course of history. Indeed, this appears to be what Russia is attempting to accomplish with its vast propaganda/information net that has spread out across Europe and offers its brand of objective reality (consider, for example, Russia's numerous failed attempts to explain, via various scenarios, how MH 17 was shot down; to them, reality is negotiable) instead of truths.

The Red Web

In 2015 two Russian authors, Andrei Soldatov and Irina Borogan, wrote a book titled *The Red Web: The Struggle between Russia's Digital Dictators and the New Online Revolutionaries*. It offers an excellent summary and background on the development of Russian information and cyber issues over the past century. The authors, who have their own website (Agentura.ru), note that the book is an investigation into what happened in their country when two forces, surveillance and control on one side and freedom on the

---

[25] Sivkov.

[26] No author listed, "Secret 'Rus' Surfaces Successfully," *Argumenty Nedeli Online (Weekly Arguments Online)*, 17 December 2015.

[27] *Interfax* (in English), 12 October 2015.

[28] Ibid.

[29] *Interfax-AVN Online*, 16 December 2015.

other, collided over digital issues.[30] *The Red Web* demonstrates how a combination of surveillance, control, mobilization, information, and manipulation are integrated to the benefit of the Kremlin.

On Control

In 1998 Russia's Federal Security Service (FSB) produced a draft document that made Russia's Internet Service Providers (ISP's) install black boxes on their lines, thereby connecting the ISP with the FSB. The black box system, which furthered control over information, was known as SORM (System of Operative Search Measures) and it became a technical means to investigate electronic networks, or to conduct eavesdropping on the Internet. It was not even mandatory for the FSB to show a warrant to anyone when it made inspections. The ISP owners were forced to pay for the black box and its installation yet they had no access to it.[31] There reportedly have been three levels of SORM over time. Soviet KGB telephone tapping was dubbed SORM-1. Internet tapping, to include Skype, was dubbed SORM-2, while SORM-3 included all telecommunications.[32]

On June 7, 2012, the Russian State Duma introduced legislation for a nationwide system of filtering on the Internet, including a single register of banned sites, i.e., a blacklist.[33] The blacklist would block Internet protocol addresses, sets of numbers, URLs, or domain names the FSB described as harmful. The Federal Agency for Supervision of Communications (Roskomnadzor) maintained the blacklist.[34] By March 2014 Russia had four official blacklists of banned websites and pages: those deemed extremist; those that included child pornography and suicide or banned drug discussions; copyright problems; and sites blocked because they called for demonstrations not approved by the authorities (and conducted without a court order). An unofficial fifth blacklist was for those sites or groups deemed to be uncooperative.[35] Putin wanted to ensure that the West would never be able to start an uprising like Arab Spring in Russia. In April 2014, he declared that the Internet was a CIA project.[36] Authorities clearly feared the Internet might be used to interfere in internal affairs, or undermine sovereignty, national security, territorial integrity, public safety, or be used to divulge information of a sensitive nature.[37]

A Template to Understand Russia's Media Control

---

[30] Andrei Soldatov and Irina Borogan, *The Red Web: The Struggle between Russia's Digital Dictators and the New Online Revolutionaries*, Public Affairs, New York, 2015, p. x.
[31] Ibid., p. 68.
[32] Ibid., p. 70.
[33] Ibid., p. 166.
[34] Ibid., p. 196.
[35] Ibid., p. 263.
[36] Ibid., p. 238.
[37] Ibid., p. 233.

Soldatov and Borogan developed a template through which to understand the Kremlin's approach to media control:

- Parliament produces a flow of repressive legislation that exploits cracks in previously published rules and regulations;
- Hacktivists and trolls attack and harass liberals online, posing as someone other than a Kremlin supporter;
- Roskomnadzor is granted the power to censor and filter the Internet;
- Kremlin-affiliated oligarchs bankroll and take over media companies;
- Specific manufacturers are selected to provide surveillance equipment;
- Putin's paranoia of enemies ties these actions together, resulting in threats and intimidation.

Putin's system is effective as long as people are certain the Kremlin is in control. This dynamic can be transformed when a crisis occurs and message are shared in real time.[38] Thus, in the end, the digital directors of the Kremlin have gotten what they wanted: a reenergized populace sympathetic to Putin's actions and convinced of Western conspiracies to neuter Russia, resulting in his exceptionally high popularity rating.

Case Study: Ukraine

There have been several countries that have allegedly been attacked by Russian hackers in the past six months that have openly discussed the incidents, with Lithuania, Latvia, and Estonia some of the most prominent. Only Ukraine is discussed here.

Before addressing several late 2015 attacks, it is important to return to the Presidential elections in Kiev in May 2014, for the necessary background. Just 72 hours before the election that potentially would offer a mandate to Ukraine's population to develop a legitimate pro-Western government, the election headquarters were hacked by a pro-Moscow group known as CyberBerkut. Fortunately operations were restored in time for the elections. CyberBerkut has also attached government documents on its website, and it has hacked the Ministry of Foreign Affairs then the Ministry of Defense, among others. CyberBerkut is allegedly an independent Ukrainian organization. Ukrainian officials, however, strongly suspect Russian involvement with the group. There is little surprise in Ukraine's weak cyber security system, since it has much Russian technology in its inventory, is infested with Russian supporters, lacks security updates, and hosts much of its e-mail on servers located in Russia. The hacker tools being used against Ukraine are sophisticated, further indicating nation-state sponsorship.[39] But there is no proof. And that is the same scenario that seems to be repeating itself in 2015.

In January and February 2015 there were Ukrainian reports that Russian special services had launched campaigns to disrupt Ukraine's mobilization effort. There were social

---

[38] Ibid., pp. 313-314.

[39] Margaret Coker and Paul Sonne, "Cyberwar's Hottest Front," *The Wall Street Journal*, 10 November 2015, pp. A1, A12.

network videos that told people to reject mobilization. Ukraine's Security Service noted that this is a campaign to force people to doubt the need for protecting their "motherland" and that it is an information and psychological operation. Their sources say that two groups of the General Staff's Main Intelligence Directorate are behind the disruption campaign. Phase one is to persuade people of a logical link between poor command, oligarch actions, and frontline problems. Sample applications were provided to help people avoid mobilization on, as the application noted, legal grounds. Phase two may involve organized protests by so-called soldier's mothers and reports about soldier funerals and torture.[40]

Thus Russia has been a bit trickier with its use of cyber against Ukraine. One Kiev report noted that there was a scheme to bribe voters with Internet technologies. As the report noted

> The cyber technology to remotely bribe voters has for the first time been used at these elections (on 25 October and mayoral runoffs in several big Ukrainian cities on 15 November). It includes several stages. At the first one, people are enticed by having their mobile phones topped up by 50 hryvnyas (about two dollars). Then those who respond are paid 400 hryvnyas for a photo of a ballot paper with a tick next to the name of an elected candidate.[41]

A member of the Interior Ministry of Ukraine stated that the funding came from Moscow. Law enforcement officials stated that 10,000 people sold their votes at the 25 October election.[42]

In December a report from iSight Partners claimed that it had gotten the malicious code that caused a massive blackout in the Ivano-Frankivsk region of Ukraine leaving hundreds of thousands of homes without power. The size of the blackout was viewed as a milestone in hacking, since in the past such attacks, which are commonplace, never caused such an incident. The country's energy minister blamed Russia for the attack on the power grid and security firm ESET agrees, since malware known as BlackEnergy caused the outage and it is a Trojan that has been used by Russia in previous attacks against Ukrainian targets.[43] Another report noted that US security agencies were studying malware from the 23 December blackout affecting nearly 700,000 homes for several hours. They had not decided if the hackers acted on behalf of Russia's government or with its implied consent.[44]

---

[40] Kiev 1+1 Television, 25 January 2015.

[41] Kiev 1+1 Television, 13 November 2015.

[42] Ibid.

[43] See http://www.cnet.com/news/cyberattack-causes-widespread-power-blackout-in-ukraine

[44] See http://thedailybeast.com/articles/2016/01/06/exclusive-cia-eyes-russian-hackers-in-blackout-attack.html

Several examples of Russia's use of reflexive control (get someone to do something for themselves that they are actually doing for you) in Ukraine (use of analogies, deception, etc.).

Russia's Intelligence Oversight Apparatus

To implement many of the arrangements above, eight agencies are reportedly permitted to conduct investigative activities in Russia: the Ministry of Internal Affairs (MVD), the Federal Security Service (FSB), Federal Protective Service, Foreign Intelligence Service (SVR, which of course investigates activities outside Russia), Customs, the Federal Drug Control Service, the Federal Corrections Service, and the MOD's Intelligence Directorate (GRU). Several of these organizations have expanded their surveillance activities as of 2012. For example, the Federal Corrections Service purchased the System of Operational and Investigative Measures (SORM) equipment, which are packages enabling one to intercept phone and Internet traffic. The law was expanded to include areas where people did community service for crimes instead of being incarcerated. It is nearly possible to wiretap an entire city.[45] Earlier the Supreme Court had upheld the Right of the FSB to wiretap oppositionists on the ground of engaging in protest activity.[46] Overall it appears that the goal of increased agency and FSB surveillance of the Internet is designed to highlight pro-Kremlin messaging and limit domestic opposition messaging and thus movements.

Military-Related Cyber/Information Reforms

During the past two years there have been several very interesting cyber developments for the MOD. In January 2014 the Chief of the General Staff's Eighth Directorate stated that Russia will create a special structure to protect critically important facilities against computer attacks.[47] In April it was reported that Roselektronika will design a supercomputer which will help testing, along with simulations. The supercomputer's processing capacity is 1.2 petaflops.[48] On May 12, 2014, an article noted that the creation of Information Operations Troops would be stopped, since it was too expensive.[49] However, only two weeks later an article described the army's creation of cyber subunits. Missions included both defense and mounting attacks. In addition to programmers, the table of organization and equipment would include highly skilled mathematicians, engineers, cryptographers, communications personnel, translators, and other supplementary specialists. This will require a center for cyber defense inside the General Staff and a cyber-defense center for each military district and fleet.[50] To date, however, no corroborating evidence has supported this contention in open source documents, other

---

[45] Andrey Soldatov and Irina Borogan, "Why Are We Now Being Monitored More?" *Yezhednevnyy Zhurnal (Daily Journal)*, 20 December 2012.

[46] Ibid., and Soldatov and Borogan in *The Red Web*.

[47] *RIA Novosti Online (RIA News Online)*, 30 January 2014.

[48] *RIA Novosti (RIA News)*, 9 April 2014. FLOPS (floating point operations per second) is a measure of a computer's processing speed. A petaflop is the equivalent of one quadrillion FLOPS.

[49] *RIA Novosti Online (RIA News Online)*, 12 May 2014.

[50] Aleksandr Stepanov, "Battle of the Computers," *Versiya (Version)*, 26 May 2014.

than the creation of a science company in Tambov dealing with cyber issues; and the desire to create two science companies of programmers.

At the Tambov science company, a military organization designed to recruit talented young programmers, students will be taught how to wage computer wars, erect barriers against Internet attacks, prevent attacks on classified networks, and impede an adversary's troop command and control and weapon use.[51] Another report on the science company stated that the new subunit will make it possible to boost the efficacy of applied-science research, testing in the EW sphere, and training of specialists, and will help in developing data protection methods.[52] In 2013 Shoygu had supported the development of a cyber-command authority,[53] but it wasn't until 2017 that the unit was officially announced.

Conceptual Views

In 2011 the MOD proposed a document known as the *Conceptual Views on the Activities of the Armed Forces of the Russian Federation in Information Space*. This document defined terms that included information warfare and information weapons, among others. *Conceptual Views* also offered principles (legality, priority, integration, interaction, cooperation, and innovation) to guide the activities of the Russian Federation's Armed Forces (RFAF) in information space.[54] The paper proposed several definitions of terms. One of the most interesting was the concept of information war, which the paper defined in the following way:

> Conflict between two or more States in information space with the goal of inflicting damage to information systems, processes, and resources, as well as to critically important structures and other structures; undermining political, economic, and social systems; carrying out mass psychological campaigns against the population of a State in order to destabilize society and the government; as well as forcing a State to make decisions in the interests of their opponents.[55]

Of interest is that this last line is nothing more than the definition of reflexive control (RC), which the Russians use to deceive decision-makers into making decisions that Russia desires. RC was defined in 1995 by Colonel S. Leonenko, who stated that RC "consists of transmitting motives and grounds from the controlling entity to the controlled system that stimulate the desired decision. The goal of RC is to prompt the enemy to make a

---

[51] Aleksandr Stepanov, "Defense Ministry Announces Recruitment for Science Troop. Students Will be Put under Cyber Arms," *MK Online (Moscow Komsomol Online)*, 6 April 2015.

[52] Anton Valagin, "The Ninth Company Will Become an Electronic One," *Rossiyskaya Gazeta Online (Russian News Online)*, 26 January 2015.

[53] Aleksey Mikhaylov and Dmitriy Balburov, "Shoygu Returns to Rogozin's Idea of Creating a Cyber Command Authority. The Defense Ministry is Preparing for a Full-Scale War in Cyber Space," *Izvestiya Online (News Online)*, 12 February 2013.

[54] "Conceptual Views on the Activities of the Armed Forces of the Russian Federation in Information Space," *Ministry of Defense of the Russian Federation*, 2011.

[55] Ibid.

decision unfavorable to himself."[56] Reflexive control can be used at the strategic or tactical level to influence decision-makers or individual citizens. It must be studied closely.

2013-Information Confrontation and Future War (Major-General Vladimir Slipchenko, whose article was published posthumously)

In the 1990s and into the first decade of 2000, Major-General Vladimir Slipchenko was one of the most prolific and creative military writers in Russia. His two most impressive works were books, those being *Future War* and *Sixth-Generation War*. His importance should not be underestimated, since after his death a leading ground force journal, *Army Journal*, published one of his articles. He noted there that information superiority includes (1) domination in space and reconnaissance systems, and in warning, navigation, meteorological, command and control, and communication assets (2) advantages in numbers of recce-strike systems and precision missiles (3) speed of introducing new programs, systems, and capabilities and (4) reliable information protection of assets.[57] Slipchenko wrote that man should expect the development of a set of various forces and means capable of disrupting the normal functioning of the planet's information domain and information assets as well as the means of life support for Earth's inhabitants. Next-generation warfare may not be focused at the operational or strategic level but at the planetary level, provoking technogenic catastrophes in large economic regions or those with information networks and assets. He wrote that after 2050 ecological weapons may also be developed for directed effects against countries' mineral and biological resources, local areas of a biosphere (atmosphere, hydrosphere, lithosphere), and climate resources.[58]

2015 Directive on a Russian Federation/People's Republic of China Agreement on International Information Security

Directive No. 788-d was dated 30 April 2015 and contained a synthesis of a Chinese-Russian cyber agreement. It contained ten articles and an annex. The articles were fundamental concepts, principal threats to information security, principal areas of cooperation, general principles of cooperation, principal forms and mechanisms of cooperation, information protection, financing, relationships to other treaties, dispute resolution, and concluding provisions. The annex defined ten terms.[59] They are: information security, infrastructure, area, resources, and protection; critical information infrastructure facilities; computer attack; illegal utilization of information resources; unsanctioned interference with information resources; and threats to information security.[60] The directive discussed threats to critical information infrastructure facilities,

---

[56] S. Leonenko, "On Reflexive Control of the Enemy," *Armeyskiy sbornik (Army Digest)*, No. 8 1995, p. 28.

[57] V. Slipchenko, "Information Resources and Information Confrontation: their Evolution, Role, and Place in Future War," *Armeyskiy Sbornik (Army Journal)*, No. 10 2013, p. 52.

[58] Ibid., p. 53.

[59] "Directive on an Agreement between the Governments of the Russian Federation and the People's Republic of China on International Information Security," *Government of the Russian Federation Website*, 13 May 2015.

[60] Ibid.

such as networks, finance, power, and so on; and it discussed the importance of illegally influencing the creation or processing of information.

Two terms that were defined are worth highlighting, information area and computer attack. An information area is "the sphere of activity associated with information creation, transformation, transmission, utilization, and storage exerting an influence on, *inter alia*, individual and social consciousness, information infrastructure [defined as the aggregate of technical facilities and systems for information creation, etc.], and information proper."[61] Thus an information area concerns itself with both information-technical (infrastructure, transmission, etc.) and information-psychological (individual and social consciousness).

An information attack is "the deliberate use of software (software and hardware) tools to target information systems, information and telecommunications networks, electrical communications networks, and industrial process automated control systems carried out for the purposes of disrupting (halting) their operation and (or) breaching the security of the information being processed by them."[62] Thus an information attack appears focused more on systems than people, although it can, of course, impact them depending on the type of messages transmitted.

Article Two considered information security threats to be constituted by the utilization of information and communications technologies for carrying out acts of aggression aimed at violating state's sovereignty, security, and territorial integrity; for inflicting economic and other harm, such as exerting a destructive impact on information infrastructure facilities; for terrorist purposes (to include the propaganda of terrorism); and for perpetrating infringement of the law and crimes, such as illegal access to computer information. Threats included the use of technologies to interfere in states' internal affairs, violate public order, inflame interethnic, interracial, and interfaith enemies, propagandize racist and xenophobic ideas and theories giving rise to hatred and discrimination and inciting violence and instability, and also to destabilize the internal political and socioeconomic situation and disrupt the governance of a state…[63]

Of special interest was that each state "shall not carry out such actions against the other Party and shall assist the other Party in the realization of the said right."[64] "Such actions" include the right to protect the states information resources against illegal utilization and unsanctioned interference, including computer attacks on them.

Conclusions

Russia is motivated by dangers and threats to its information space, whether they be political, economic, military, diplomatic, or others. Software writers and their teams, along with a thriving hacker and troll community, continue to cause problems for the West. Russia's military aims to further enhance reform by introducing high-tech equipment into

---

[61] Ibid.
[62] Ibid.
[63] Ibid.
[64] Ibid.

the military. As Defense Minister Shoygu stated, words, cameras, photos, the Internet, and other types of information can become weapons on their own. These weapons can serve, in the hands of an investigator, prosecutor, or judge, Shoygu notes, as elements that change the course of history.

Meanwhile, the FSB and other intelligence services will continue to control the population's online activities; to engage the international community in developing a cyber-code of conduct or to influence events abroad; and to prevent "color revolutions" from breaking out in Russia. Suspicion of the West will, it appears, continue to dominate security thinking.

Mr. Timothy L. Thomas

TIMOTHY L. THOMAS is a senior analyst at the Foreign Military Studies Office at Ft. Leavenworth, KS. He conducts extensive research and publishing in the areas of peacekeeping, information war, psychological operations, low intensity conflict, and political-military affairs. He is an adjunct professor at the U.S. Army's Eurasian Institute; an adjunct lecturer at the U.S. Air Force Special Operations School; and a member of two Russian organizations, the Academy of International Information and the Academy of Natural Sciences. Mr. Thomas was a U.S. Army foreign area officer who specialized in Soviet/Russian studies. His military assignments included serving as the Director of Soviet Studies at the U.S. Army Russian Institute in Garmisch, Germany; as an inspector of Soviet tactical operations under the Commission on Security and Cooperation in Europe; and as a brigade S-2 and company commander in the 82nd Airborne Division.

Mr. Thomas has written six books on information warfare topics, focusing on recent developments in China and Russia.

Mr. Thomas holds a B.S. in engineering science from the U.S. Military Academy, and an M.I.R. from the University of Southern California.

QUESTIONS SUBMITTED BY MEMBERS POST HEARING

MARCH 15, 2017

Mr. FRANKS. If we are to take seriously the threat posed by Russian, Chinese, and jihadi information operations seriously, is the GEC the appropriate institution to combat these aggressive (and successful) information operation strategies? What reforms or changes should be made to the GEC to make it more effective—or should we create a new entity for this mission?

Mr. ARMSTRONG. Thank you for this question. The informational element is not a sideshow. It is at the heart of international affairs. The kinetic effect of a bullet or bomb is often secondary to the informational effect. At its core, terrorism is an informational act. Our adversaries, from Russia to China to Iran to ISIS, understand that success in the informational, or more specifically the psychological or cognitive, domain is central to a successful offensive and defense. We must begin to accept this reality.

The GEC was established as an interagency hub within the State Department to provide a point of leadership—and accountability—for the Government's response to adversarial information activities. The majority of the staff are from the interagency—mostly from the Defense Department—with few from the State Department. Its ability to coordinate, let alone affect and effect, actions within the State Department and the interagency is limited.

The GEC has and continues to face resistance from elements within the Department that perceive GEC as not a part of the Department's mission. Several functional and geographic bureaus do not understand or accept how the GEC supports the Department. The reasons are numerous: an ossified State Department bureaucracy and operational culture; confusion over the Department's role in national security; questions over authorities, questions on what tactics may and should be used; and, a remarkable lack of leadership support from outside of GEC, including from past Secretaries, senior staff, and other Under and Assistant Secretaries.

These challenges will not be irrelevant by creating yet another new entity without addressing the fundamentals that led to the creation of CSCC and GEC, based on a faulty vision of tactics and poorly defined mission, both of which limited any possible effectiveness. These same barriers caused ripples that negatively influenced interagency partners' willingness to work with and support the GEC. At this time, there are no indications that any of the GEC's limitations have been removed or will be soon.

The function of an organization like GEC (though GEC's mission, in all aspects, is too narrowly defined) should remain inside the State Department. The expeditionary, long-term approach of the State Department, it's ground presence in nearly every nation on the planet, and its fundamental role in our foreign policy and national security makes the Department the best location for an operation like the GEC.

I have two recommendations. They are not exclusive in that they may, and should, be pursued simultaneously.

First, there is an existing operational and integrative hub for global informational and in-person engagement in the Department: the Under Secretary for Public Diplomacy and Public Affairs. However, only one of the eight persons to hold the office since it was established in 1999 (the office has been vacant for nearly 30% of the time since then), none have been adequately prepared, directed, or supported to fulfill a role of coordinating, integrating, and supporting U.S. Government-wide global engagement. An Under Secretary will wield substantially greater influence than a "coordinator" or "Special Envoy." This existing Under Secretary has direct or indirect control over a nearly $1b budget, which contains the bulk of the USIA's former informational (short-term and long-term) engagement capabilities. However, this Under Secretary faces similar redundancies and turf-protecting (and building) that the GEC met, and has done so without leadership support to overcome these limits to better support our foreign policy, national security, and support to interagency partners for the same.

Congress must address the systemic deficiencies at the State Department as it is the right home for the required hub. The original Portman-Murphy proposal in the Senate was intriguing as it could have been a spark to cause a substantial reconsideration of the poor organization, misalignment, and disconnectedness of various overlapping Department efforts while undoing the forced segregation of "information" from the rest of national security and foreign policy structures and bureaucratic cultures.

I am not aware of a single Congressional hearing or clear mandate by a Secretary of State or President to empower and hold accountable this Under Secretary to fulfill the role embedded in it when it was created following the abolishment of USIA in 1999. The GEC, like the Center for Strategic Counterterrorism Communication it replaced, and the Portman-Murphy bill proposed in the last Congress, are direct responses to the failure of this Under Secretary to perform a function too many have forgotten it is positioned and resourced to execute.

Second, I recommend the Congress reconsider the "Political West Point" idea of an organization that provides analysis and training for adversarial informational activities that State Department, Defense Department, and other agencies, as well as relevant private sector and friendly nation governments and civil society actors, can attend. The name for this "Political West Point" was the Freedom Academy when it was introduced in Congress in the late 1950s, though a different name may be useful today. Such an organization would address the underlying resistance derived from a denial that information is anything but a sideshow to the other three core elements of national power: Diplomacy, Military, and Economic. The "D," "M," and "E" are not coequal with the "I" of information, but rely on Information for their effect. Further, on the military side, the lack of appreciation of the centrality of informational activities have permitted, if not encouraged, military public affairs officers to aggressively segregate themselves, and their advice, from the military's trained information professionals. At the State Department, this will help break down the cultural divide between the Public Diplomacy cone (where "cone" is the Department's loose equivalent the military's "MOS") that information is a key facet of international affairs. It would also benefit the military through an increase informational training for MOSs not directly involved in information (i.e. look beyond Information Operations, Psychological Operations, and Civil Affairs), as would other agencies, from Agriculture to Treasury to AID. This would provide some of the analytical support GEC presently strives to deliver, and operate similar to and likely with West Point's Combating Terrorism Center. This Academy would be a repository for the collection and analysis and training on adversarial tactics, techniques, and procedures across the psychological and cognitive domains, including the cross-over to the physical domain.

Thank you for the opportunity to respond to the question. I look forward to discussing this issue in greater detail with you.

Mr. FRANKS. If we are to take seriously the threat posed by Russian, Chinese, and jihadi information operations seriously, is the GEC the appropriate institution to combat these aggressive (and successful) information operation strategies? What reforms or changes should be made to the GEC to make it more effective—or should we create a new entity for this mission?

Mr. LUMPKIN. The GEC is currently the most viable institution in the Executive Branch of government to lead and direct efforts to counter the threat posed by Russian, Chinese, and Jihadi information operations. That said, the GEC continues to face significant challenges to fully realize its potential in addressing these threats. Insufficient funding, manpower, and support coupled with the thick bureaucratic layers at the State Department have historically hampered effective operations.

Four principle things can be done to make the GEC significantly more effective:

1. Increase funding to the GEC and provide it a dedicated funding line.
2. Significantly increase the assigned manpower.
3. Elevate the GEC in status at both the Department of State and within the Interagency and authorize it to "direct" U.S. government efforts to counter both State and non-State actor threats in the information environment.
4. Ensure the GEC has aggressive leadership with a proven track record of success operating in the interagency.

Mr. FRANKS. What specific steps must we take to combat Russian hybrid warfare? Do we ultimately need to oppose them at every stage? For example, if we merely park armored brigade combat teams in Eastern Europe but do not improve our cyber capabilities or harden our space assets, will Russia be deterred?

Mr. THOMAS. The basis for my response utilizes contemporary Russian open source military thought, and not the mirror-imaging of U.S. concepts onto Russian activities, which is the type of analysis many U.S. analysts incorporate. Russia's military leaders state often that it is the U.S. who developed the term hybrid war, and it is the U.S. who is using this concept to confront Russia. Westerners, on the other hand, state that Russia is using hybrid techniques. The Russians themselves state that they tend to depend on "new-type" warfare methods, the outline of which is attached [see graphic below]. Russia's chief of its Main Operations Directorate stated in 2015 that "nonstandard forms and methods are being developed for the employment of our Armed Forces, which will make it possible to level the enemy's technological superiority. For this, the features of the preparation and conduct of new-type warfare are being fully used and 'asymmetric' methods of confronting the enemy are being developed." After determining vulnerable areas, Special Forces, foreign agents, information effects, and other nonmilitary forms of effects are used in each conflict, with each involving a different set of asymmetric operations (coordinated with respect to targets, location, and time, a combination of asymmetric and indirect actions)."

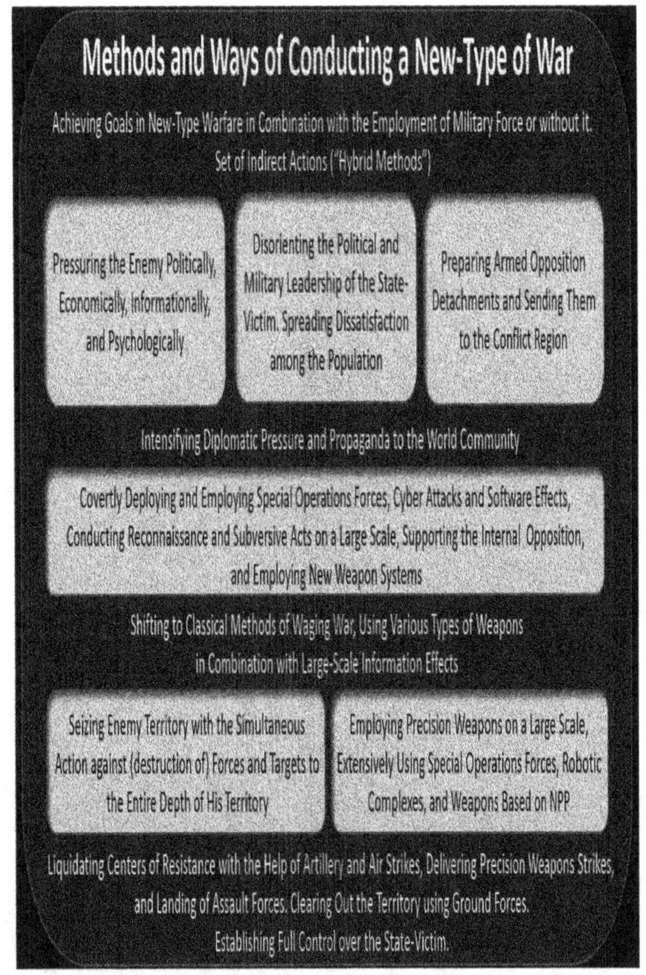

Russia's new-type warfare method has several apparent phases (none of which are numbered) that ratchet up confrontations incrementally. The U.S. should confront Russia at every stage of this template and attempt to ensure the phase involving classical war methods is never reached. The initial phase of new-type warfare would be the best time to confront Russia, when we are only dealing with various types of deterrence methods (information, psychological, etc.), diplomatic pressure, and propaganda means before actual confrontation evolves. We are clearly in this phase now, which involves posturing and threats. We should do all in our power not to move beyond this phase. However, if this phase fails, then new-type war's next phase involves the covert deployment of special operations forces and cyber-attacks, and the use of heretofore unnamed types of new weapons systems. This would be a real step toward actual fighting and the absolute last chance before, according to the Russian General Staff's new-type warfare scenario, classical warfare methods begin. As long as President Putin views an existential threat to Russia, I do not believe that Armored Brigades in Eastern Europe will deter him, nor will hardening space assets. He will find a way to asymmetrically, as the Russian military has stated, threaten the U.S. Perhaps these ways have already been prepared and are ready for use or exploitation. I do not believe he wants his military to conduct combat operations against NATO or the U.S., but I also believe he is prepared to use them if necessary. Of recent importance is that a major discussion of the term "war" is underway among Russia's military elite. This debate must be followed closely as perhaps new types of warfare methods are under serious consideration. For example, the military's emphasis on "nonstandard," "asymmetric," and "nonmilitary" methods should be watched closely for indications of their future application in war. The views expressed in this response are my own and do not necessarily reflect the views of the Department of the Army or Department of Defense—Mr. Timothy Thomas.